In the San Juan

Colorado

Sketches

By
Rev. J. J. Gibbons

A REPRINT BY
WESTERN REFLECTIONS PUBLISHING COMPANY
LAKE CITY, COLORADO

A Reprint Published by
Western Reflections Publishing Company
P.O. Box 1149
951 N. Highway 149
Lake City, Colorado 81235

www.westernreflectionspub.com
westref@montrose.net

Copyright Western Reflections Publishing Company 2008
All rights reserved including the rights to reproduction in
whole or in part.

Printed in the United States of America

Library of Congress Number 2008924068

ISBN 978-1-932738-62-9

PROLOGUE

Father J. J. Gibbons was a pioneer Catholic priest in early Colorado, who endured many hardships while carrying his faith to the people of the region. His book, *In the San Juan*, deals with the time he spent in the San Juan Mountains of Southwestern, Colorado. Father Gibbons received his assignment to the Town of Ouray, Colorado, as a result of the Catholics of that town buying Ouray's original Presbyterian church building and offering it to Colorado's Catholic diocese if a priest would be provided. At about the same time, the Catholic priest serving Montrose, Colorado, complained to his superiors that he had been "kidnapped" by Ouray ladies who had made him hear their confessions for over six straight hours. In response, famous pioneer bishop, Joseph Machebeuf, assigned Father Lawrence Haton to the Ouray church in 1886, but two years later the church was turned over to Father Gibbons.

Father Gibbons was born in Providence, Rhode Island, moved to Wisconsin as an infant, and grew up in Iowa, where he attended St. Francis School in Dubuque. He attended St. Mary's seminary in Baltimore, was assigned to Chicago, and then was sent to the missionary diocese of Colorado, where he served for forty-five years.

In 1885, he was assigned to Georgetown, Colorado, then Silver Plume (where he only served two months), and then Leadville. Shortly after he arrived in Leadville, a serious epidemic broke out in the town, and Father Gibbons worked around the clock tending to the sick and dying and holding funerals.

Father Gibbons was one of the first Catholic priests to venture into the rugged San Juan Mountains during the area's rough and tumble mining days. He was assigned to Ouray and Silverton in 1888, but lived in Ouray. He also had twenty missions that he was responsible for in the San Juans.

Because of the size and ruggedness of his assignment, Father Gibbons was constantly on the go – coping with all types of weather, using all kinds of transportation, and becoming involved in some extraordinary events. After just four years, the exhausted young priest left the area for less arduous tasks. He went first to Denver, then back to Leadville, and then to Barnum. He died at Mercy Hospital in Denver on December 3, 1931.

In the San Juan, originally self-published by Father Gibbons and only covering the time that he was assigned to Ouray, certainly is a testament to his faith. Yet, it is also an extraordinary glimpse into life in the San Juans during the heyday of silver mining. Stories of skeletons along the trail, miners blown to bits while warming dynamite on a stove (this was actually a common practice when dynamite froze), and powerful avalanches known as the white death, are just a few of the many true tales related by the intrepid priest in this wonderful book.

Western Reflections is honored to bring this historical work back into the public eye so all can enjoy, through Father Gibbons' words and pictures, a time long past.

P. David Smith

Publisher

In the San Juan

Colorado

SKETCHES

By
REV. J. J. GIBBONS

COPYRIGHT, 1898
BY
REV. J. J. GIBBONS

CONTENTS

FIRST SKETCH

Page

FIRST EXPERIENCES IN THE SAN JUAN—Land of mountains and plains—Home of the Cliff-Dwellers—Mummy apostrophized—Trip to Telluride—Young Canadian falls over a precipice—A flourishing mining camp—Silverton in Christmas attire—The "Gloria in Excelsis"—The sacred strains in the midnight air—Perilous night ride. - - - - - 7–25

SECOND SKETCH

FUNERAL IN THE ROCKIES—A daring and expert horseman—The cowboy and the wild broncho—Sensational drilling contest—Chattanooga's two inhabitants—Sunset on Ophir's range—Disaster befalls a tenderfoot—Skeleton recalls a tragedy—"Marry in haste, and repent at leisure"—Mountains echo the "Requiescant in pace"—A sudden storm. - - - - 26–38

THIRD SKETCH

FROM DALLAS TO TELLURIDE—A genial stage-driver—A hero of the Crimea—Fatal accident at the Sheridan—A picturesque canon—Dreadful catastrophes—Train of burros—Sequel of right line movement—Religious services at Telluride—Summoned in haste to a deathbed. 39–55

FOURTH SKETCH

A SOCIAL AND RELIGIOUS CENTER—Hospitable family on the Divide—Pastoral scene—Excursion party in the interests of science and religion—A few shots from a rifle bring relief in

CONTENTS

Page

a dilemma—Medicine administered at the point of a gun—Sick call to Turkey Creek—An invalid and his queer nurse—Curiosity punished—Navajo Indian—Trout Lake, a romantic spot—Fifty-five miles in the saddle. - - 56–71

FIFTH SKETCH

CELEBRATION OF A FESTIVAL—An unhappy marriage—Bear Creek Falls festooned with snow—The Mother Cline snowslide—Ironton's unique character—Hairbreadth escape in a storm—Racy ballad, "Patrick's Day in the Morning"—Sick-bed conversions—The hospital, from a missionary standpoint. - - - - 72–83

SIXTH SKETCH

THRILLING INCIDENTS OF A HUNTING TRIP—Superior qualities of the broncho—Breakneck race down cork screw trail—The deer that never came—The Cascade of Ouray—Mountain scenery at its best—The bear and the prospectors—"The burnt child dreads the fire"—The mountain lion—The Snowslide in verse--Perplexing situation—The welcome stream—Home again. 84–103

SEVENTH SKETCH

A DEVOTED MOTHER IN ADVERSITY—A captain meets reverses of fortune—Sad deathbed scene—Manual and Industrial training of the young—Education in the right line—Solemn religious service at early morn—By the Hermosa—A red-haired stranger—A "friend in need is a friend indeed"—Strange chorus in a storm—Verses on the burro, "He's a bird—a true canary." - - - - - 104–119

EIGHTH SKETCH

THE BLASPHEMER'S FATE—Some of Ouray's sociable characters—Life above timber line—Appalling misfortune—Prince, the beautiful setter—Faithful friends lost in an avalanche—

CONTENTS

Page

Edifying death of a miner—Told in verses by a local poet. - - - - - 120–137

"Only the Actions of the Just,
Smell sweet and blossom in the dust."

NINTH SKETCH

BANEFUL EFFECTS OF INTEMPERANCE—John, the soldier—Spending a fortune— "Nothing heavenly in the miser"—A promising career ruined by drink—Reflections upon the evils of intemperance—Triumph of grace—Reconciliation —"All's well that ends well." - - 138–153

TENTH SKETCH

TEN DAYS ON A SICK CALL—Old Gray, the horse with one ear—On a hogback—Dolores and the early missionaries—Attending a sick man under difficulties—A tidy bachelor's hall—Dies on his way to the lowlands—How funeral expenses were defrayed—A mail carrier, faithful in death —Ingenious use made of an ulster. - 154–166

ELEVENTH SKETCH

VIRTUE, THE ONLY NOBILITY—The boys of Donegal—Pleasant companions on a stagecoach—Rico's second boom—Telluride's bank robbery—Sheriff's posse in pursuit of robbers—Baptism at the Springs—Weird scene at early dawn—Death's lesson. - - - - 167–182

TWELFTH SKETCH

COLORADO AMONG THE STATES—Her people and her resources—San Juan's future—A great city of the southwest—"Fountain of Perpetual Youth"—Las Animas canon—Sublime scenery —How a mine is worked—A miner's mode of living—His intelligence—A land "where the peach and apple grow"—Ouray, the Picturesque. - - - - 183–194

PRESS OF
CALUMET BOOK & ENGRAVING CO.
168 S. Clinton Street,
CHICAGO.

FIRST SKETCH

IN August, 1888, I received my appointment to the parish of Ouray, which included pretty nearly the whole of the San Juan country, the scene of these sketches. San Juan is the familiar designation of southwestern Colorado. Bounded on the north by rugged ranges, on the south by New Mexico, on the east by the Gunnison district and on the west by Utah's Blue mountains; it is a mountainous country, diversified by rolling uplands, smiling valleys, darkling glens and rushing streams.

When, as a traveler from the east and on my way to Colorado to enter upon my duties as a priest of the diocese of Denver, the Rocky mountains burst on my vision, Pike's Peak appeared like a sentinel at the gateway of a new world. For the flat plains which mark a thousand miles' travel from the Missouri, I beheld scenes of inspiring grandeur. My fancy pictured the condition of a society where cities and towns lie in the clouds, and people live in the presence of perpetual snow and cutting frosts that penetrate the earth to a depth of six or seven feet. I had read of mines, sunk thousands of feet into the bowels of the earth, and of railroads overhanging dizzy abysses. I had not been long in this wonderland, however, when I got some inkling of the kind of life men live at this great altitude, for I experienced the pleasures of a renewed vitality and the clearness of a quickened brain. "Land of illusions and magnificent distances," cries the newcomer — where the atmosphere is so rare that to visit before breakfast the foothills, twenty miles from Denver, seems nothing extraordinary, and where, upon mountain loops, the railroad passenger of the rear car may well be tempted to light his cigar at the headlight of the locomotive.

From the time of my arrival in Colorado, I was engaged in pastoral work at Georgetown and Leadville, until I was sent to my southwestern mission. It was an extensive one, covering a territory perhaps as large as the whole of Ireland. It was not uncommon to be summoned day or night to sick calls, involving trips of 150 miles.

The aboriginal inhabitants of this country, the Cliff-Dwellers, belong to a race of men who built houses of solid masonry, or chiseled caves in cliffs, that seemed unapproachable. When Coronado, 350 years ago, explored New Mexico and the great region which contained my new charge, he discovered towns with populations varying from 10,000 to 40,000. The people tilled the soil, built adobe houses as well as more pretentious structures of cut stone, raised cotton and made their own clothes; they owned large herds of cattle, and the rich valleys bore maize and vegetables of many kinds. Being virtuous, they were happy, they kept the natural law and paid religious homage to the sun from their round towers at early dawn. To those simple children of nature, the orb of day, which is the light-giver and the heat-bringer, was the chief object of adoration, and in their bountiful harvests they recognized his secondary action under Providence. They were, to be sure, ignorant of the true God; but their idolatry was pure and intellectual, compared with the gross

THE CLIFF-DWELLERS

worship of nations that adored crocodiles, leeks and onions. Like the Persians they were fire-worshipers, and therefore elevated in their aspirations. Were they of Celtic origin? Perhaps they were; I do not think the most rabid advocate of an alliance, offensive and defensive, between Uncle Sam and John Bull, would claim that they were Anglo-Saxons. Did they come from Egypt, the land of some lost arts? They were a people of culture; for their pottery, architecture, agriculture, argue considerable progress in the arts and sciences. Their origin and history being veiled by the twilight of fable, it is not easy to say anything definite about them; but that they practised cremation is evident from the fact that charcoal in abundance has been found in their graves. It is certain that they wrapped their dead in well-woven garments and deposited the bodies in caves or tombs set apart for that purpose. Several well-preserved skeletons have been discovered, still clad in their burial robes, the skin dried and shrunken upon the bones, but retaining the natural features, thus furnishing some clue to the past of a wonderful race. Indeed, the lineaments of the face, the flowing black hair, the long sharp nose, the desiccated body suggest the mummy, which let me, *a la Poe*, interrogate:

> Say, mummy grim, tell me I pray,
> From what mysterious land you came?
> Was it from where fair Eden lay,
> And Eve acquir'd her hapless fame?
> Your very face denies disguise,
> And plainly tells of Afric's skies;
> Your straight black hair and olive hue
> Bespeak your race.—Th' Egytian Jew?
> Your forehead's high, your face is clean,

IN THE SAN JUAN

Your caste's proclaimed in princely mien,
The home-spun round your limbs made fast
Suggest your culture to the last.
I ask not for your royal name:
But tell me, prithee, whence you came?
Was it in Noah's ark you went,
And viewed the rainbow, Heaven-sent;
Dreading storms on Ararat bleak,
True comfort here you came to seek,
And high in cliffs, from perils free,
You built those houses we now see?
Your pitchers bright may still be seen,
Artistic, tipped with glowing sheen;
The pots remain, the kettles too,
The race is gone, but who are you?
Did you go forth from Abram's band,
When God spoke of the promised land?
Or o'er the sea 'neath pillar's light,
When Moses saved from Pharaoh's might?
The manna, quails, the serpent's bite
Are facts historic in your sight.
I crave thee, tell us of your past,
For we're a nation living fast;
We thirst to know the how, the when,
The why, the that, the thus, the then.
Perhaps you're of a later age,
I'll jog your mem'ry with a page.
Did you e'er hear of Christ, the King
Of whom seers speak and angels sing,
Beth'lem's stable, the winter's night,
The shepherds' vision, Joseph's flight,
How water blushed e'en as he willed,
The loaves increased, the storm stilled,
The sick were healed, the demons fled
And men arose that erst were dead;
How for mankind His love to show
He suffered death, its pain and woe?
Twenty of centuries—long space—
Have changed in much the human race,
While kingdoms, empires, rose and fell,
Writ in sanguine hues, hist'ries tell.
Years gone by, your mist-wrapped land
Columbus viewed, with cross in hand;
From Manco's plains and canons deep
Came Francis' sons with you to weep.

FIRST EXPERIENCES

> They found not man. On shelving rock,
> Your doors were hingeless, broke the lock,
> The corn untouched, the embers black,
> Sole relics of your nation's track.
> This land espied on western wave
> Is now the fair home of the brave,
> Whom despot rulers could not hold,
> Here live in bliss like kings of old,
> Serve the true God, enjoy their days
> Compete in art and social ways.
> Nature's dim veil they've deftly rent
> And heaven's fire to uses bent;
> The facile 'phone with ready sound
> Conveys the news the country round,
> The stately bike dots road and glen
> Where women ride the same as men;
> The phonograph, artistic scheme,
> Keeps the speech of an ancient theme.
> Had your ancestors saved its din,
> We'd have your story, kith and kin;
> We might describe your early fate,
> Learn the myst'ries of Behrings strait.
> No answer make you, nought you'll tell,
> Good bye, queer mummy—fare thee well.

In my new parish there were only two churches, one at Ouray, the other at Silverton, twenty-seven miles distant. There were twenty missions or stations, with new ones springing up, as mines were discovered, saw mills put up, or families settled on the mesas, west of the San Miguel river. Having assumed my charge in the latter part of summer, I had ample time to visit all the stations before the winter set in. Tom Knowles, who kept a hotel at Ouray, paid me a ceremonious call on my arrival, and invited me to take a horse and saddle whenever I wished. It was a liberal act, for hay was worth from eighteen to twenty dollars a ton, and grain was always high. I availed myself of his kind invitation. My first trip was to Telluride, and my mission was to baptize a descendant of Kosciusko and Brian Boru, a young Margowski. The roads were good, and the most squeamish could make the trip without special risk of life or limb, save on the top of the pass at an elevation of 13,000 feet. Here, for 300 yards you were compelled to take a trail that was always slippery from the constantly thawing snow, which fell nearly every time there was a storm. The snow, however, remained in the shady crannies of the rocks, melted during the day, and trickling down the narrow path, froze at night. Along the left of the trail was a steep precipice, and I noticed far down on a plain of rock several dead horses; but at the time I never thought of horses falling and rolling a quarter of a mile over the rocks. In going up the narrow trail my horse came to his knees several times, and, feeling unsafe, I dismounted and walked up the way leading to the pass. The trip to Telluride was made without an accident, but on my return about two inches of snow covered the ice on the pass. My horse's shoes were not sharp, and he fell before we had descended the mountain twenty-five yards. For ten minutes I paused to consider what course I should take. I concluded that I could not follow the trail, so I went down the side of the mountain, led my horse, and took chances. Scarcely had I turned from the trail five yards when a mass of snow, ice, mud and loose rock began to move down the mountain, and we moved with it. It was a sort of locomotion we had not bargained for, and the situation was such as to make the horse tremble with fear and greatly disturb me. At last, with much watchfulness and care in keeping our feet, we arrived safe on the rocky plateau below. A young man who, I subsequently learned, was from Connecticut, was just coming up the trail on his way to Telluride. He asked me about the trail, as it was barely visible over the broken rocks. I informed him that unless his horse was well shod and the shoes sharp, it would be the height of folly to continue his journey, but the stranger would make the attempt. I went on; and, as I was on the point of crossing the ridge of rocks that separates the Virginius mine from the pass, I looked back and saw the young man close to the top of the range, making slow progress. The horse was slipping, and I sat upon a rock to watch developments. When within ten yards of the pass the horse fell, rolled off the trail and shot down the mountain like a rocket. The young man threw up his hands in terror and it was well for him that he was not in the saddle at the time. The horse must have tumbled for a quarter of a mile among the jagged rocks, and I presume every bone in his body was broken. I continued my journey, having learned a useful lesson, never to ride a poor horse, or one not properly shod.

The success of my first year in the San Juan would have been greater, had the conditions of the parish been more favorable to harmonious action. Misunderstandings will arise in the best regulated societies, and to realize to fruitful purpose the divine constitution of the church, which distinguishes the teaching from the hearing element, needs a good will more than scholastic acquirements. As order, which is heaven's first law, requires this distinction, it follows that when the subject undertakes to teach the superior how to discharge his duties, nothing but confusion prevails. "But heresies must be that the approved may be made manifest."

It had been snowing for three days before Christmas, and crossing the range was no holiday pastime; but as Silverton was in my jurisdiction, I resolved to brave the danger, say the midnight mass there on Christmas night, and on horseback return to Ouray, where I intended to say two masses on Christmas day, which happened that year to fall on Tuesday. Accordingly, I left the previous Saturday for Silverton, where I said mass on Sunday. I had arranged with a gentleman, named Fred Thornton, that he was to come over on Christmas eve with two horses from Ouray, not only to test the trail, but to consider the feasibility of our returning after the midnight mass, for, as there was no night stage running between the two towns, I should be obliged to return on horseback. Fred was an expert horseman and an old mountaineer. I discovered after his death that he had a history of his own, as well as another name. He had been in the regular service in the Far West. One day while with a companion watching the horses and mules some distance from camp, the Indians swooped down upon them. The boys sprang to their horses and made good their escape for a long distance; Fred had the better horse and outran his companion, whom the Indians overtook and killed not far from camp. Fred rode in and gave the alarm, having left his companion to die alone. The soldiers regarded this as an act of cowardice in Fred and despised him. Fred often spoke to me of his hairbreadth escape and claimed that he too would have been killed had he attempted to make a stand. He concluded that discretion was the better part of valor and saved himself. It was after Fred's death, which happened a year later, that I learned his real name was not Thornton, and the probability is that one bright morning he bade Uncle Sam goodbye. Fred was no coward; several bullet marks in his body, received in actual combat with the Sioux and Commanche Indians, attested his valor. Of a good family, fine personal appearance, gentlemanly deportment, religious temperament, moreover, a capital shot, Fred was born to command.

I made the trip to Silverton on Saturday morning in the usual way by stage without any more serious inconvenience than that of finding myself obliged to shovel snow, open the road and help drag out the horses from the high drifts. Napoleon's trip across the Alps may be considered pleasant when compared with the fatigue and perils of a journey away up in the clouds during one of the fierce storms which sweep through the canons. At times it is hard to tell which way the wind blows; it comes at once from all points and so thick is the fine sifted snow that you are almost blinded. Besides, midway down in the canon on the narrow road drilled in the side of the mountain out of the solid rock, with 2,000 feet of giddy heights above and a depth of 3,000 feet below, the mind is filled with consternation and dismay at the boding terrors around. But though the arrows of death fell around me, I was safe; for the Lord was my helper. The novice is so alarmed at the sight of the abysses around him that even in the summer, when the roads are good and danger is remote, he alights from the coach and prefers to walk, not trusting himself to the best vehicle and driver. The scenery baffles description—sublime and awful alone can describe it. In the winter only old stagers and people habituated to mountain travel will essay the road. A false step, a small snowslide, and an act of contrition is in order.

There was much travel in those days, as the mines at, and in the vicinity of, Red Mountain were producing much ore; and, besides, the boys often came down to the metropolis of the San Juan to enjoy its famous baths and get a box of Doctor Rowan's pills. This worthy son of Æsculapius had a specific for all diseases under the sun and threatened to send every one who did not use his spring medicines, about the time the ground-hog showed himself, to Rowan's ranch, which in local parlance meant the graveyard. Two of the boys came down one day and, it is said, indulged over-much at a resort of unsavory reputation. Late in the evening they left for Ironton, but one of them never arrived there. The road follows the circuitous canon and it tested all the genius of Otto Mears, the pathmaker of the West, to construct it; it went east and it went west, it twisted and turned and boxed the compass, and on a dark night it would perplex the most wide-awake traveler to know what to do on this road. The two young men walked together for some time; soon one, a Canadian, began to lag behind, so the other pushed on and left his companion. The latter, in rounding one of the points, forgot to make the necessary turn and walked deliberately over one of the most awful precipices in the Rockies. Where he struck the first protruding rock must have been 1,500 feet below, and his swift flight downward was traced by shreds of his clothing; nor did he stop there, but on, down the dreadful abyss he shot, striking here and there, bounding from rock to rock, until at last in a direct sweep of a thousand feet he was dashed into the creek below. Was he killed? I should think so; not a bone in his body was left unbroken, and the very boots were torn from his feet. The naked eye could not discern him from the road at that depth, where he lay for days until men came down from the mine to hunt him up. After a long search they discovered the mangled form, which they decently buried at the Ouray cemetery.

There are some remarkable instances in the traditional history of Ouray which show that a man may fall a great distance into a canon and not be killed. For one such exception at least I can vouch. For two years as I went up and down the road I saw the remains of the wreck lying in the bottom of the canon, and there is every reason to believe that some of the sleigh box is still there. The accident happened to two miners whose names I have forgotten. They had been at Ouray over night, and in the morning left for Red Mountain on King's stage with Ike Stephens as driver, as good a Jehu as ever cracked a whip over a six-horse coach. Ike was a "peach" and would stay with the horses to the last. It had been snowing a little, but it was a pretty fair morning when Ike pulled out for Red Mountain, with a big load of eggs and general merchandise, and for his live freight, the two miners who made up their minds not to go home until morning. They occupied the back seat in the sleigh. Just as they were rounding the last dangerous point before coming by the numerous small slides that always came down when it stormed, the accident to which I refer occurred. On the cliff above there were two spires of rock that shot up for many feet. The snow drifted in between these and down upon the road, forming a high bank, over which Ike had the temerity to drive. The consequence was that when the sleigh went down over the ridge of snow, the box came from between the sleigh stakes and started over the precipice, the horses plunged forward, Ike held on to the reins and the now frightened leaders drew him out of the box, but the miners, the eggs and dead pigs, together with a large amount of merchandise, went over and fell nearly a straight 250 feet. Strange to say not a bone was broken; the two men escaped with a few scratches and a big scare, but the box was in flitters. It was no smooth slide—it was a sheer fall straight down until they came within twenty feet of the bottom, and then a tumble of about the same distance into the creek. The miners were in an india-rubber condition when they realized where they were and resolved the next time to go home before regular bed time. I had a little personal experience, coming down the same road from Ironton. To the left are two little lakes. Old Joe was the driver and could handle four horses as well as any man on the line. He had a soft spot in his heart for me and always tried to make me as comfortable as possible. The driver's seat was a coveted place; unless some drummer from Denver monopolized it very early in the morning, old Joe to all inquiries would reply "this seat is taken," for he knew my day to go out. We left at the usual time for Ironton, whither I was bound, to see after the building of a church. On the return trip a large excursion party was making the circle and there were many passengers from New York and Boston. Joe had a light stage and the two wheel horses of the Concord coach attached to it. I sat by his side and we were enjoying the grand scenery when the nigh horse shied at a piece of wood in the roadway. The horse, which was a powerful animal, crowded his mate over to the edge of the bank in spite of Joe's hard pulling. I reached out my right hand, caught the lines and drew the horse's head back to the harness saddle; it was too late, we were gone. The stage turned completely over and slid down the embankment through the brushwood and rock. The horses fell and tumbled over and over, I held on to one rein and Joe to the other, a lady screamed and a gentleman from the Hub lost his hat, exhibiting a bare head that would provoke an Irishman's shillelah on a fair day in Ireland. The spring seat seemed to catch the inspiration, for it struck him fair on the exposed part and opened the scalp fully four inches. I fared no better, for the tire on the wheel struck me below the knee, fracturing the bone and scraping me to the ankle. The horses tried to walk over us, but crippled though we were, we managed to control the animals and get the wagon on the road. We were happy to reach Ouray alive. In compensation for the accident, the stage owners politely furnished me with a pass over the road. Those days are gone, and their associations of mingled pleasure and pain, but the pass still remains. I had many thrilling experiences on these perilous roads, but I passed through the ordeal unscathed and with an increase of valuable knowledge. The missionary has many sources of consolation, when he observes in the scene of his labors the wondrous operations of grace as well as nature. While his labors are many, the balance in the comparison of his vocation with that of other men is in his favor. Even here below he enjoys blessings a hundred fold, and he has the promise of a special crown in the future to nerve him in the battle of the present life.

We arrived about one o'clock at Silverton, very little worse for a rather exciting trip. During the afternoon I called upon most of the families in town, and notified them that on Sunday we should have not only mass, but benediction of the Blessed Sacrament and a Christmas midnight mass. Mrs. Prosser had charge of the choir and was a musician of no mean degree. A convert, intelligent, pious and charitable, she was active in promoting Catholicity in that mining camp. The Silverton church workers were second to none in the state, and, strange to say, were nearly all women. Practical woman suffrage was in wholesome operation there long before it was embodied in the legislation of the state. The women attended not only to the proper duties of the altar society, but in no small measure to the financial affairs of the church. Fairs and balls were organized and managed by them, the tickets were sold, the collections made and the money put in the bank to the credit of the church. I am happy to know that their zeal has not abated, for word comes still that they are not weary of well doing. I said that the

FIRST EXPERIENCES

church workers were, strange to say, nearly all women, for I do not forget that representative Catholic gentleman at Silverton, Barney O'Driscoll. Who does not know Barney O'Driscoll of the San Juan? Who has not heard of him in the state of Colorado? Honored by his district with a seat in the councils of his state, Barney has always worked for the best interests of his constituents. Familiarly styled the colonel, he is known of all men. A military man as well as a lawyer, he served in the Civil war, after which he drifted with hundreds of others into the San Juan. He has lectured in most of the towns of the southwest on politics, the Bible and science, mineralogy and all the live subjects of the day. Until his grandchildren grew to a sufficient size to wait on the altar, the colonel served mass every Sunday, and as long as he was around the camp the priest did not shovel snow from the church door, or build a fire when the thermometer was twenty-five below zero. Upon my arrival at Silverton the colonel sought me out at once and looked upon it as a crime if I remained at the hotel. He loved to treat me with the best southern hospitality, and ransacked the butcher shop for the tenderest of the toughest Kansas chickens and the freshest of the stalest Kansas eggs, which found their way into the mountain camps. If I was not at the colonel's I could be found at Lonergans', Cramers', Higgins', Prossers'; indeed, the people of Silverton felt deeply offended, if I declined their hospitality.

On this particular Sunday before Christmas, the colonel waited, as was his wont, after mass to escort me to his log cabin, which stood some distance from the church, at the base of a mountain that towers on the north far above the little city, which nestles in its shelter. The lofty peaks were hidden in clouds; dense mists swept over them now and again, and streaks of light illuminating the darkness, revealed the shifting storm, which was raging on the summit of the mountain. The colonel shook his head and said: "You will have a hard trip across the range tomorrow night." A good dinner at his hospitable board caused me to forget the pangs of a long fast and the thought of impending dangers. At three o'clock, on returning to the church, we found that it had narrowly escaped destruction in our absence. The candle which I had left burning before the Blessed Sacrament, emitted a spark which set the altar cloth on fire, and the fire went out just when the cloth was burned from the epistle side to the front of the tabernacle. The colonel was in favor of pronouncing it a miracle, but at all events, the church was safe and we felt happy.

Little Joe, the colonel's nephew, then saddled his famous burro, and fetched two large loads of green spruce and pine for the Christmas night decoration. The next day every one helped to beautify the altar and the church. Boughs of green were conspicuous everywhere. With the paper roses that had been made by the ladies of the altar society we decked the pine—strange it was to see American beauties on pine trees, but the simple artists thought the effect was good and there were no others to be satisfied. About five in the afternoon Fred Thornton arrived from Ouray with the horses, which we were to ride back after midnight mass. His report on the condition of the trail was discouraging. It was heavy, in part filled, and the mountains so much covered with snow, that snowslides might come down at any minute. I spent the evening hearing confessions, instructing the children and at intervals watching the finishing touches that were given to the altar. At twelve o'clock the church was filled to the doors with Protestants as well as Catholics. It is customary for the miner to come to town at least three times a year, at Christmas, Easter tide and on the Fourth of July, and if he is a practical Catholic, the church is one of the first places he visits. At Christmas, the town is alive with the hardy sons of toil, who gather from far and near to replenish the empty grub sack and buy powder and other necessaries for the winter siege in prospect. Most of the boys were in church that night, and there was a regular round of hand shaking and merry Christmas greetings before and after the services. A little after twelve the "Gloria in Excelsis" pealed through the little fane and was caught up by the choir until it rang out in sweet strains of music far up the streets of the town. I preached a short discourse on the Christmas holy day and the lessons that should be drawn from the event. I was unable to extend my remarks, as I had to set out for Ouray immediately after the services. The service over, Fred soon had the two horses before the church door. We sprang into the saddle and many a God speed and merry Christmas followed us into the storm and wind. We were soon rounding Stoibers' mill and heading up the valley to Red Mountain. The night was dark and a sifting snow filled the air, making it necessary to go slowly and feel the way. At the mill there were

IN THE SAN JUAN

several trails. Unfortunately we took the wrong one and found ourselves crossing to the opposite side of the valley. We endeavored to turn in the narrow passage, where our horses floundered in four feet of snow. After a while they fell, compelling us to dismount, tramp the snow and give them a chance to rise. When we regained the old trail close to the railroad track, I told Fred to follow me on the track to Red Mountain. I had learned from a miner who had ridden down the track on Sunday, that the trail was fairly good. I knew there were no trains, the bridges were few, and we hoped in some way to get over them. Far up the height for a mile or more the snow enveloped the mountain, and the danger of a snowslide was great. When we reached a place where twenty or thirty mules, and I believe a man, were lost, several years before, we were struck with fear and Fred said afterwards that while passing it he could scarcely breathe; but no slide came down. At times we walked to keep up the circulation in our benumbed limbs and rest our wearied horses, and then, leaping into the saddle, spurred our animals on, hoping to reach Ouray by seven o'clock, the time set for the first mass. At Sheridan Junction we left the railroad along which we had been steering our way and resumed the trail, which proved to be a good sleigh road from that to Red Mountain. Fred took a hot cup of coffee and it must have been strong, as he was more lively the rest of the trip, which, to the gratification of our jaded horses, was down hill. When we entered the canon it was still dark and rendered more so by the snow which was falling and drifting. All at once my horse stopped and

FIRST EXPERIENCES

refused to move. I urged him, but he stood stock still, then I struck him, and suddenly turning, he tried to walk into the canon. I wrenched him back with all my might and, dismounting, saw to my horror that there was a high snow bank across the road and that the horse, unable to go through it, had been trying to go around it. We should have been precipitated to the bottom of one of the most awful canons in the Rockies, had the horse pursued the way upon which I was urging him. Breaking a path through the drift we were in the saddle again and another hour brought us into Ouray on time for the second mass, chilled to the bone and worn out. I proceeded to say my other two masses and was soon feasting on a breakfast of the American bird.

SECOND SKETCH

IT is a true, if flippant, saying of the political orator, that people are certain of two things in this world, namely: taxes and death. The latter is not so prevalent as the former in the greater altitudes, owing perhaps to the fact that few who have passed the meridian of life, attempt any considerable elevation. Death, however, comes and beckons the young and strong to its cold embrace here as elsewhere, with the same imperious finger as those whose life is already on the wane.

One Saturday afternoon in the early autumn of 1890, I received a despatch from Silverton, notifying me that Mrs. —— was dead, and that my presence was required at the funeral, the following afternoon. Silverton is twenty-seven miles from Ouray, and beyond a lofty range of mountains. Thirteen miles of the journey are up hill and fourteen down. On Sunday I was to say mass at Ouray at 9:30 a. m. and at Red Mountain at noon. Red Mountain camp was on the top of the range, 11,000 feet above sea level. In 1890 it was in the heyday of its glory. Everyone had work, and if I remember aright the wages was three dollars and fifty cents a day. It was easier to get money than specimens of the peacock and ruby silver, which came from the famous Yankee Girl, a million-a-year producer hard by. The Vanderbilt and Genesee, a few hundred yards distant, were also big shippers of gold as well as silver, and the town was in a flourishing state. The lights never went out in the camp, unless when coal oil failed, or a stray cowboy shot up the town. The men worked night and day, shift and shift about, and the people were happy. The gambling halls were never closed, the restaurants did a profitable business, and no one could lay his weary bones on a bed for less than a dollar. Whiskey was as plentiful as the limpid water that gushed from the hills behind the town, sparkling in the sunlight. In those days it never cost a stranger anything for drinks; he was welcome to eat, drink and be merry; indeed, it was deemed an insult to refuse to partake of anything that was going. Tramps were as scarce as Indians on the shores of Long Island. The prospector's cabin on the mountain trail was left unlocked. You might step in, cook your dinner and go on, or if tired, unroll your blankets and rest to your heart's content. If the owner was at home it was all right, if not, the conditions of hospitality were the same, and these were, "come in, help yourself, and go rejoicing on your way,"—a striking contrast to great cities, where a selfish opulence drives the needy from the door. The owner of the mountain cabin, free with his money, bacon or bunk, deemed it an honor to entertain his caller, however poor. Should the reader ask of what nationality such generous people were, the answer is Americans, Irish-Americans and Irish. In my work on the missions, I have found Americans liberal and self sacrificing, and I do not believe that I have any prejudice in their favor, because I was born beneath the folds of the Star Spangled Banner. Of the Irish and the Irish-Americans there can be only one opinion, and it is, that in the masses you will find the two extremes, the worst and the best.

They are great in faith, hope and charity when they are good; but when they are bad they are bad all over. The four little churches, whose bells call the people to divine worship from Ridgeway on the north, to Silverton on the south, a distance apart of forty miles, tell of their faith. With their own hands and money we toiled together, until at every ten miles of the way a bell hailed the name of Mary, Joseph or Patrick. There was no church at that time at Red Mountain; later one was erected two miles below at a little town called Ironton. The schoolhouse, an old store, or a private residence, served as a place of worship, and the priest always received a warm welcome from the miners, who never failed to drop their mite into the basket on Sunday. A five or ten dollar bill or coin was nothing strange to find in the collection. The miner said, "He made a good talk and we ought to help the preacher." I said mass at Ouray at the usual time on Sunday morning, preached a short discourse on the gospel of the day, and was about to mount my broncho for Red Mountain, when I espied my old friend Billy Maher, who had just come down from Mount Sneffles, where he had been working in the mines. I invited him to accompany me to Red Mountain, and fulfil the precept of hearing mass on Sunday. Billy assented and hastened to the livery stable for a horse, there to find only one wicked broncho whose heel leverage was known far and wide. This animal had the centre of gravity so well focussed that he could buck a Kansas cowboy out of the saddle, or give a Navajo Indian a pain in the midriff for a week. But Billy, nothing daunted, ordered him saddled and brought out.

All the stable boys in King's barn tightened the saddle girth at the imminent risk of their lives, and the famous roan was led forth. Billy vaulted into the saddle with all the grace of one of Sherman's troopers. In the twinkling of an eye the horse stood on his hind feet as if to depart to the world of spirits, and then came down, with his fore feet stiff upon the ground, with a thud that would break the heart of an ordinary man; in another moment his hind feet were far in the air and his head was bowed low, throwing Billy well forward in the saddle; but the familiar half grin remained on the face of the rider, who sat like a rock on a mountain. Billy was an athlete. Born at the foot of Keeper's Hill in Tipperary, he came of a hardy peasantry that know no fear. He had often ridden his father's gray mare over hedge and ditch in the hunting season, keeping well up with the hounds, so he was quite in his element. Half Ouray was out, and the gamblers deserted the faro tables to see the sport outdoors, for everyone knew, and, what was better, esteemed Billy Maher, the man that never swore, never drank to excess, never lost his temper and had a good word for everyone. Billy, too, was the right hand man of the priest and sisters. Many a time he led the sisters over the rugged mountain passes, and from camp to camp, gathered the dollars that helped to build the hospitals of Durango and Ouray. But to return to his encounter with the broncho. The animal gradually stopped its wild plunging and dashed madly up the street, everyone getting out of its way for bare life. Here, for the moment, let me digress to mention the characteristic feat of the expert cowboy subduing the wild broncho. The wild pony is led out into the street, the throngs cheer, the horse, unused to man, becomes frantic and strives to break away. When everything is ready, the sprinter of the plains is turned loose and stands for a moment perplexed, looks wildly around and then rushes down the street with lightning speed. With a whoop the cowboy is after him, and when the wild horse has attained his greatest speed, the cowboy rises gracefully in his stirrups, measures the distance between himself and the fleeing pony with his eye, then his arm shoots out, his hand poises in the air and a coil of rope unrolls like a serpent, hastens on its course with unerring accuracy, catches the hind foot of the frightened horse and closes around it. In an instant the trained horse of the cowboy throws himself back on his haunches, planting his fore feet firmly on the ground to meet the resilient shock which comes, when his foe is stretched upon the ground. An ordinary rider would go far over the horse's head, but the cowboy is prepared for the rebound and remains firmly seated in his saddle. The lassoed horse is laid low by a dextrous movement and in an instant the cowboy is out of his saddle and has a bridle on the animal. The other pony keeps the rope taut and stands, viewing the ceremony with great interest. It takes but a few moments to put a saddle on the animal and then the fun really begins. The handling of the bucking broncho is an amusement which makes the most sedate laugh, and success in the operation crowns the rider who holds his seat ever after as a victor. The antics of the horse are ludicrous, dangerous and even foreign to that noblest of animals. In trying to get rid of the rider, it will lie down and roll over

VIEW ON OURAY TOLL ROAD

if possible. Rising on its hind feet, it often falls backward and maims or kills the rider. Jumping stiff-legged, crossing its feet, kicking, striking with its fore feet or springing into the air and coming down solidly on the ground, are feats which delight the cowboy. Gradually its powers of endurance are exhausted and the animal becoming docile, learns to love the cowboy.

We were off at last and at a speed that would have dazzled the eyes of the hero of Winchester. The road for eight miles is narrow, with barely room for two teams in the widest place. You can see the bed of the creek two thousand feet below. By the time the most dangerous point was reached, Billy's horse had cooled down and was quiet and gentle. A grade of three thousand five hundred feet in thirteen miles deserves mention even in the Rockies, and when we arrived at Red Mountain our horses were not in the best shape. Billy brought the boys together, and I arranged the temporary altar, beginning mass at about 12:30 a. m. When breakfast was over I had a pleasant chat with those patient delvers in the bowels of the earth, and an introduction to the newcomers in camp. Mutual good will exists among the poor and honest sons of toil, and in a marked degree this is true of the miner, who always lives in danger of death in handling dynamite. Moreover, he runs the frequent risk of being maimed for life by premature explosions, caving-in of mines and breaking of cables. Whether this has anything to do with the miner's frankness and good nature I know not; but I have seen more genuine sorrow exhibited over a miner, killed in an accident, than at the pompous funeral of the elite. I have found a

IN THE SAN JUAN

warmth of feeling in the grasp of a finger-stalled hand that I have never experienced in the kid-gloved touch of the city cad. The miner's ways are characterized by simplicity, bluntness and honesty, and he possesses a rough, sound, practical judgment. Even his pastimes evince a marked degree of virility. Witness the drill contests. They are the supreme final test of superiority among the picked hammer strikers and drill turners, and cause such excitement in a camp that thousands of dollars change hands. Great muscular power and endurance is something of which any one may be proud. For months before the trial, two or three hours are spent each week in periods of fifteen minutes, and these giants of the drill stand over the hardest block of granite that can be found in the mountains. One of them strikes the drill for three or five minutes and the other turns it; a good turner, again, is an absolute condition for success, for if the drill once becomes fast in the rock, the contest is practically over. The drill must have received the proper temper and the blows must come with a force proportioned to the strength of the drill. The blows fall like a trip hammer and with a rapidity which the eye can scarcely follow, and with each blow the drill turns in the hand of the holder, ejecting the fine-cut granite from the hole, and thus keeping it open. At the end of a few minutes, the striker, fatigued by his rapid movements, drops the heavy hammer into the hands of his companion, seizes the drill and the hole goes down into the hardest of granite at the rate of an inch and a-half to the minute. Twenty-five inches or more have been drilled into the granite in a quarter of an hour, something which our fathers thought, never could be accomplished by the hand of man. While he makes little display of piety, he is firm in the faith and ready to do what is fair. He will not fight without a good cause, and he does not need much of the diplomatist's art to decide when he is in the right. As a rule, he minds his own affairs, and except when he indulges over much in the cup that inebriates, keeps out of strife and cares, and, therefore, is entitled to wear a medal on his breast.

Billy having answered many questions about the boys on the stormy mountains, we tightened our saddle girths, mounted our bronchos and rode leisurely down through the tall pines to the dilapidated town of Chattanooga. It had been dismantled by a snowslide which a few years before swept away a part of the town, and its condition at our visit was not inviting from any point of view. The ruins, consisting of the roofs and sides of houses, were strewn for half a mile over the valley, and the population of a once flourishing hamlet had dwindled down to the small number of two. One of these kept a saloon, which was a sort of half-way house between Red Mountain and Silverton. The other, who was a widow with many children, appeared to be in the laundry business, for the clothes lines were always full; but where she got her customers the future historian of Chattanooga must discover. The afternoon was beautiful. The sun sent his slanting rays down the Ophir Range, diffusing them in quivering banners of light, until they reached the valley below, where they were lost in a maze of shadows. The aspen far up the rugged heights, "confessing the gentlest breeze," was just changing into the sere and yellow leaf of the dying year. The sides of the mountain, clothed in the purple hues of scrubby oak leaf and flora, indigenous to the state of Colorado, and adorned with a bouquet here and there of pine or spruce, offered a delightful picture to the lover of the wild and romantic in nature. As noble a stream as ever burst from Colorado's mountains rushes on forever to the smiling valley; rocks like cathedral spires, towering sky high, pierced the azure dome of heaven, and one peak soaring far above the others seems to stand like a sentry over the glorious creation. The blue canopy rests like a curtain on the valley, while the deep hush of the autumn afternoon invited the mind to reflections upon the Almighty Artist, who reveals Himself in such an awe-inspiring manner.

Here we had to ford the stream at the old crossing. We drew up our jaded horses to let them drink of the cool water. To the right, upon a little knoll, lay the whitened bones of a horse, stripped clean by coyotes, mountain lions and years of bleaching in a rarefied atmosphere. Billy said musingly: "Father Gibbons, that horse has a history. If those bones could speak, they might tell of a tragedy which happened at this crossing and in this stream. When the rich strikes around Silverton were made, people rushed from all quarters to the new El Dorado, some to work, others to gamble and many to see the wild West; but all to make a fortune at once. Among them was a youth of refined education and manners. I have forgotten his name, but for convenience sake, I shall call him Tom. Tom came to the camp to get rich, but, like many others, he found out that gold does not grow on the trees. The long winter in Silverton kept him from prospecting in the mountains, and, like many of his young acquaintances, he spent no small part of his days and nights in dissipation. By degrees he became as depraved as any of the vicious classes of the frontier. He was an expert gambler and drank deep of the draught that kills. The dance hall and the wine room made him a physical and moral wreck. He cast aside the wholesome restraints of religion, and the influences of early training lost all their force for him. One night he played for high stakes with a man of few words and a cool head, one who kept an eye on his opponent as well as the cards. Of course the trusty forty-five lay beside the heap of gold, that shone in the lamplight of the dingy gambling house. It is said that Tom cheated, and was called down; there was a fight and the trouble was patched up by the onlookers and the parties themselves. After this the game dragged along in silence, but a silence that was so intense and significant as to suggest an undercurrent of unpleasant feeling, notably in the taciturn stranger. When daylight came they were about even in the game, and the man of reserved manners, walking up to the bar, invited all the company to have a drink. Then turning to Tom, he said: 'Let us go over to Red Mountain to-morrow. I am tired of this place.' 'All right,' said Tom, 'after dinner, we shall go.' So after dinner next day they left Silverton for Red Mountain, and here at the crossing they gave their horses a drink, just as we have done. Poor Tom was a little in advance of the stranger, who, while the horses were drinking, coolly drew his

revolver and deliberately shot his companion dead. With a groan Tom dropped from the saddle into the icy water, and his horse rushed through the stream to the opposite side. Another well-directed shot from the murderer's pistol laid the horse low upon that little knoll, and his bones have remained there all these years."
Billy and I spurred on our horses and were soon in front of the neat little white church, which stood like an angel at the foot of the mountain.

The funeral to which I had been summoned was already at the church, which was tastefully draped by the good ladies of Silverton. The deceased Mrs. —— was a lady of good birth, a woman who, an American would say, had a great deal of push and energy. She had come to this country young, but with a mind well stored with Catholic doctrine. She had acquired the rudiments of her education in the national schools of Ireland, which afford the young an excellent training, and received the finishing touches of a liberal education in a convent school. In a moment of folly she contracted an alliance with one who, in station and culture, was her inferior, and reaped the fruits of her imprudence in an unhappy married life. With true Christian patience she accepted the cross, nursed her grief in secret, and with her vision purified by suffering, learned to accept her lot and acknowledge that it was just. Thus her domestic trials were for her the discipline of perfection, and being a faithful child of the church, "she learned obedience by the things she suffered." In a letter which I received after her death, she left the story of her sorrows in an impassioned narrative that would draw tears from the most hardened. She

FUNERAL IN THE ROCKIES

revealed the skeleton that was hid in the closet, and as I reflected upon her death, which, humanly speaking, was untimely, the thought came to me that it might have been better for the poor creature if she had spent her life in her mother's modest cottage than as the wife of a domestic tyrant, who hated the Catholic Church and compelled his devoted wife secretly to steal into the house of God to worship Him after the fashion of her ancestors. But she married a stranger to the household of faith. She did not live in vain, however, if her example serves as a warning to others. The last prayers having been said, the funeral cortege moved through the little town to the cemetery, where the final benediction was given. As the mountain breezes softly fanned the newly made grave, and bore away the echoes of the murmuring *requiescant in pace*, we turned from the sad scene with sobering thoughts upon the vanity of earthly things.

The sun was just below the mountains and we had an opportunity of enjoying one of the splendid sunsets for which Colorado is famous. No poet's pen or artist's pencil could give the faintest idea of that sea of golden light in which the monarch of day sank to his rest, bequeathing the glowing radiance of his departure to the mighty ranges. With one of the sudden changes which are familiar in these regions, the blaze of glory had scarcely faded when ominous clouds began to steal over the lately sun-tipped heights and the lazy rumblings of distant thunder warned us of the coming storm. Billy must report for work in the Virginius mine the next morning, and twenty-seven miles in the saddle surely give a man an appetite. So having fed the horses and taken a pretty substantial supper, we started homeward in good form. Passing out of the valley we began to climb the rugged ascent to Red Mountain and had not proceeded far when the rain came down in torrents. The water began to flood the trail, which we found ourselves obliged to leave and seek the shelter of a cabin, that nestled among the trees. In moving down the slippery passage, my horse fell; luckily I was not in the saddle, having dismounted before we began to climb the hill. The horse rolled down until he came in contact with a pine, around which his feet slid, leaving him in a most embarrassing position—perfectly helpless. He could not get up, he could not get down; meanwhile the rain came fast and furious. The lightning played around our heads and heaven's artillery awoke the echoes with responsive detonations, which produced a grand but terrific music. There the horse lay unable to extricate himself, while Billy and myself tugged and pulled and tried to lift, but could not move him. At last we took the halters, tied them around the prostrate animal and then to the saddlehorn of Billy's roan and detached the horse from the tree without further trouble. The storm had passed and the moon, stealing out from behind the clouds, lighted our way through the dark pines. Leading our fagged horses, we trudged over the slippery road until we arrived at Red Mountain, where we took a light lunch. After a short rest we rode down the mountain to Ouray, which we reached shortly before midnight.

THIRD SKETCH

THE winter of 1888 in the San Juan was pleasant. There had been a thaw in January, but Washington's birthday found the snow hard and compact, and the weather was fine to the end of February. Some days were so warm that the snow melted a little, even on the tops of the mountains, but froze again; thus the fear of snowslides was removed.

The miners, on horseback or afoot, had crossed and recrossed the Sneffles range on their way to the city of Telluride. They esteemed such methods of travel cheaper than to pay seven dollars to ride in the cold on one of Wood's large stages, and listen to the monotonous *bu-u-u-ing* of a stage driver, who had plied his whip for forty years over western hills and plains. Wrapped in blankets, and seated generally alone on a high seat, on a cold day, anyone might well fall into the habit of bu-u-u-ing. The old gentleman may have thought his soft humming helped the horses; but it became so much a matter of course with him, that the moment the wheels began to revolve, the tiresome refrain was struck up and held with a dreary iteration from station to station.

From Dallas to Telluride, a distance of some fifty miles, three stations provided the necessary relays. These stages were among the best equipped in the West. The horses were in good condition, well fed and well groomed, and being strong animals, whirled the stage over the road at a rattling gait. At one of the stations was an old hostler, always clean and neat, who stood six feet in his stockings, was as straight as an arrow and had a military bearing. His name was O'Connell; but it did not need the name to tell his nationality. With the approach of the stage, he had fresh horses promptly at hand and ready to put into the traces. Seldom over three minutes were occupied in the change. Everything around the lonely stable on the mountain road was as bright as a pin, and I concluded that Mr. O'Connell must have belonged at one time to Systematic Uncle Sam's cavalry. Upon hearing his name called I sidled up to him, and opened my great coat that he might see my collar and learn that I too was enrolled in a great service. I remarked in a bantering way: "That name of yours proclaims you a German, does it not?" "Oh no, Father, I was born in Ireland." "You are a Catholic then," I said. "Well, yes, Father, I am a Catholic, but it is quite a little bit since I was in a church." "When were you at your duty last," I inquired. "A long time ago indeed," he replied. "When I 'listed, and went to the Crimean War, I bethink myself I went to my duty. Then when the war was over I came to the States, and here I 'listed in the regulars, and when the Civil war broke out I 'listed once more and went to the front. I served all through the war, and got kind of careless, but I promise you I'll go to my duty pretty soon, for I'm getting to be a pretty old man now." His words were prophetic; for a few months after, he got the pneumonia. At the time of his illness, chancing to be on the stage, I visited him, and administered to him the last sacraments. Not long after he died.

On the 21st of February I received from Telluride a summons to come across the range early the next morning, to attend a funeral of a miner named Flannigan, who had been killed at the Sheridan mine. The telegram stated that two horses would meet me at the Sheridan, which is in Marshall Basin. I mention this circumstance by way of explanation, as we could ride our horses only to the Virginius mine, then go afoot to the top of the range, and down two or three miles to the Sheridan. I feared the trip, but there was no alternative. I had to cross the range as the stage had departed, and it was over fifty miles around the Sneffles range to Telluride. Fred Thornton was then at the hospital, fully recovered from a fit of sickness, and he offered to accompany me on the journey. I resolved to take my vestments, that I might be enabled to say mass. We ordered two horses for three in the morning, which was an early hour for a trip in midwinter. We packed the vestments and set the alarm clock for three; but being at that time troubled with insomnia, I slept little. At two o'clock we arose, and Fred took a light breakfast. We were soon on our way to Mount Sneffles. The morning was clear, and the mercury recorded twenty below zero. The road to the Virginius mine was in tolerably good condition. Far up the canon, however, it was somewhat dangerous on account of its closeness to the precipice, a false step, and horse and rider would be hurled two thousand feet below. Almost on the apex of the range, in the Sneffles District, the Humbolt mine is situated. The mountains stretch away from it toward the south in the form of a vast amphitheatre until they reach Red Mountain, where they turn to the north, seeming to terminate in those giant peaks, that rise up to the east of Ouray. The eye may easily outline this sublime scene from Sneffles' highest point, trace the black curling smoke as it ascends from the smoke stacks at the Yankee Girl mine, and take in, at a glance, the whole country for miles around. Old Mount Abram, gray and dull colored from the heat and storms of thousands of years, towers above all his fellows, and appears but a rifle shot down to the Ouray toll road; yet it is many miles distant.

The Humbolt is exposed to all the rigors of the winter storms on those lofty mountains. No trees or sheltering gulches break the force of the awful blizzards which sweep along those naked heights. To witness a snowslide within a short distance of the miners' bunkhouse is no rare occurrence. Mr. M—— was the foreman of this mine, and prided himself on being nearer the spirit land than most men, the Humbolt being at an elevation of about 13,000 feet. He was a miner of long experience; and, under his direction, the mine rapidly developed into one of the largest producers of that district. Before the fall in the price of silver, this mine gave employment to 180 men. A well-beaten trail connected the mine with Porter's. Every day long trains of burros might be seen moving up and down the trail, the former bringing in supplies and the latter carrying down the argentiferous treasures to Ouray. The storms were at times so severe that even the most hardy miner dared not attempt a trip to town. On one side the route for a greater part of the way led along the edge of an embankment, while on the other, high cliffs extended to the summit of the range. During a severe storm the incautious traveler is apt to lose the trail; and, wandering over the cliffs, runs the risk of being hurled to destruction. One day a Swede set out over this trail in a blinding snow storm. Losing his way, he wandered for some time among the cliffs, vainly endeavoring to find the trail. So filled was the air with thickly falling snow that it became impossible for him to know the direction in which he was going. He walked off into the abyss, and fell down the jagged rocks for a distance of about five hundred feet. The rocks, being covered with frozen snow, afforded him no opportunity of clinging to the jutting crags; so that, when once in motion, he shot down with almost meteoric speed. He lay there for many hours suffering excruciating torments, and would have frozen to death had not some miners, who chanced to be passing by, beheld, far down in the gulch, in the white snow, a dark object which they made out to be a man. By using the greatest caution, and after much difficulty, they reached him. He was in a state of unconsciousness, his skull being fractured, and his body a bruised and bleeding mass. Calling to their aid some more help, the unfortunate man was taken to the sisters' hospital, where he died in a few days.

The canon in the Sneffles' district is perhaps one of the grandest and most picturesque sights in Colorado. A few hundred yards from the entrance is Ouray. Here also the canon to Red Mountain opens, cutting a mighty seam through the granite formation. Far down in those unexplored depths, two noble streams dash along and commingle their waters in the suburbs of the city. This stream is called the Uncompaghre. As you

swing around the turn on the way to Mount
Sneffles, you behold to the right the bubbling
stream rise from the rocks. Springs of hot water
gush forth not two hundred yards from the swift
current, the icy touch of which chills the marrow
of one's bones. To the left, and far away up the
heights, tall rocks, like the minarets of a Moslem
temple, stand out in relief to the rough, serrated
points and wooded plateaus that were strewn
around when the earth was in course of eruption.
Often on a summer's afternoon have I taken my
glasses and watched the leader of a band of Rocky
Mountain sheep, as he stood upon one of
those high points keeping guard, while the others
took their meal. It was the shepherd watching
his flock, and there for hours he stood immovable,
with his eye on the road below and the city of
Ouray. These animals live near timber line,
like the chamois of Switzerland, far from the
haunts of man, and eat the small bunches of
grass that shoot from the crevices of the rocks.
They are very timid, and only an expert can come
within rifle range of them. When closely pursued they will not hesitate a moment to jump
from twenty-five to thirty feet down on the solid
rock. Coyotes, wolves and eagles, as well as the
banned sportsman, so prey upon them, that few
bunches of them now remain.

The canon is bold, grand and rugged from the
beginning. At the opening are a few garden
patches, on which, even at so great an altitude, a
variety of vegetables may be raised. In summer
the hillsides are banked with mountain flowers,
not known by the inhabitants of the valley. The
pine, spruce and poplar provide a cool shade in
the summer heats. On either side of the stream

narrow gulches pierce this deep defile, from which issue crystal streams of cold water. The scene is impressive and the sound of the rushing waters, blended with the song of the wild bird, produces a melody which soothes and delights. The farther you move up the canon, the wilder and more sublime the scene becomes. Gradually the pine and the spruce disappear and you stand upon a desert of rock with here and there a little patch of grass kept alive in the scanty soil, washed in by the rain. At Porter's, there is a valley of a few acres surrounded by pines. Porter's was then and is yet, I believe, the terminus of the wagon road. Here is the celebrated Revenue Tunnel cut into the mountain, which rises to a height of over 12,500 feet. At this elevation is the Virginius mine, one of the richest silver properties in the world. The shaft was down about 1,100 feet, with tunnels in every hundred feet. The vein is a true fissure and it was presumed that it went down indefinitely. This tunnel was designed to cut the shaft of the Virginius at 2,000 feet or more and all the veins that lay in the course. Much expense was saved in this way, and ore was shipped with less inconvenience. It was the design of the owners, by moving down the boarding houses, and placing them on a level with Porter's, to diminish the dangers of snowslides. The whole plant was to be worked by electricity, which was beginning to be used in mines as a matter of economy. I understand the tunnel has been completed to the satisfaction of the company, which will ship silver by the ton when the free coinage of the white metal becomes an accomplished fact. While few accidents attended the

IN THE SAN JUAN

construction of the tunnel, there was one in which I played a rather conspicuous part and at the early hour of two, one winter's morning. A telephone message reached me, announcing that three men had been seriously injured in a mining disaster, and were calling for the priest and the doctor. Doctor Rowan and myself, together with the undertaker and several packhorses, started for the scene of the accident. The road was in very bad shape, having been blocked for some time. By using great care we got through in the dark without injury, and found two men killed and one badly wounded. It appeared that three men, Robinson, Maloney and Big Paddy Burns were loading holes, before retiring from their shift, when an explosion occurred. The two former were over the holes and Paddy had just put down a box of dynamite at the breast of the tunnel, when, without a moment's warning, the dynamite went off, decapitating Robinson and exposing his lungs to view. Maloney was struck over the eye by a piece of rock, which was forced through the skull, and his brains were oozing out. Big Paddy Burns, who was standing at Maloney's side, was knocked down, receiving a shower of rock canister in the side of the head. He thought he was killed, and bellowed lustily for the priest. The men who were around gave him a stimulant to keep him alive, until the priest arrived. Paddy, however, bewailed his sad fate, keeping up the monotonous cry: "I'm dead, I'm dead. Why did I not die at home with my father?" This cry reached my ears when I hurried in to see Paddy. I said, "There is nothing the matter with you; come, no more of this." The poor fellow was seriously hurt, but the strength of his voice showed that he was far from being dead. That night we removed him to the hospital, where he remained six months, during which time a splinter now and then worked its way out of the skull to the great amusement of the boys and the dismay of Paddy. Finally, he left the hospital and the mountains, too, and went back to the north of Ireland, where I trust the faith he kept so well in this country will grow with the years to come.

Fred and myself arrived at Porter's safe and sound. Day was just breaking and a keen wind was sweeping down from the heights. From Porter's to the Virginius there is a burro trail, which is not wide enough for a horse, especially when going up a mountain, heavily loaded. Swaying from side to side and stumbling now and again, the animal must rest every few yards for the rarity of the atmosphere and the abruptness of the ascent. This zigzag manner of moving makes the distance to the summit three times that of the air line. The snow was very deep. If the horse stepped off the well-beaten burro track, he was sure to go down, carrying the rider with him, and once on the roll, it was hard to tell where he would stop.

We got along fairly well, until we came within a mile of the Virginius. The higher we rose, the colder it grew, and a chilling blast came over the bare heights, filling the path with a fine searching snow. Fred was in the lead and carried the vestments. I had the chalice and other necessaries stowed away behind me on my saddle in a small hand grip. Fred came to a place which was full of drifted snow. Alighting, he tramped out a path for the horse as nearly as possible in the old trail, and began to lead the animal over it. When nearly over the bad place, the horse stepped off the trail, went down to his neck, floundered a little, and lay there. We tried to make him rise, but he would not budge. At last we put a rope around his neck, which I pulled, Fred taking him by the tail, and we slid him over the danger spot and got him to his feet. Meanwhile my horse was eying the operation, as he stood quiet on the trail. Just as I approached him, about to take the reins and lead him over, one of his fore feet slipped from the path on the up-hill side. I pulled him back, but as I pulled too hard he missed the trail and lopped over on the other side. He made a tremendous effort to regain his feet, threw his head high and fell backwards down the mountain. I let the reins go and he shot down over and over, breaking through the frozen snow and missing a large stump by about a foot. Down the mountain side he sped, crossing the trail two hundred yards from where I was and recrossing it a hundred yards further down; he stopped about twenty feet from the trail, up to his neck in snow. He turned around and tried to come back to the trail, but after a few fruitless efforts to release himself lay down. Fred said to me, "You might as well shoot him, you cannot get him back on the trail again, besides I think he is badly hurt." But I did not believe it and so we went down the mountain. The horse was uninjured, and neighed at our approach. We tramped the snow and moved him a short distance; then putting a rope around his neck I got behind a tree and pulled, while Fred pushed, and by this means we brought the animal close to the trail. Then, unsaddling him, we put the saddle blanket under his feet and finally hauled him on to the trail. There we tied him to a tree, and upon examining the grip found the chalice bent but not broken; whereupon, letting the horse loose, we turned him back to Porter's and we on foot went up to the Virginius. The other horse we drove before us with the vestments and our overcoats tied upon the saddle. We were glad to reach solid ground by eight o'clock that morning. We turned the horse over to the care of the packers, instructing them to take him back to Porter's, where they were to feed both horses until the next day, when we expected to return from Telluride.

After a brief rest, we resumed our journey. Back of the Virginius the mountain rises at an angle of over forty-five degrees. Up, then, this almost inaccessible height, which at that season of the year was very slippery, were two heavy men climbing, heavily burdened and puffing like whales. We held on for dear life at every step on the glary mountain side. During the January thaw several men had come over the range, and, sinking in the snow, left great holes, which proved to be of much service to us, for by taking hold of the edges and putting our feet in the old tracks we were enabled to scramble along with some sense of security. From time to time we rested for a moment and calculated the distance we had to make. After much backing and filling, we arrived at the top, coming out on a desert of broken rocks where the antediluvian Titans played base ball with mighty boulders and, mayhap, employed the chain gang of the day in working out their fines. After another pause of short duration for rest and inspection of our surroundings, we sat on the snow and looked down on the Sheridan mine, which seemed to be within a stone's throw; but the distance down that hillside in the light atmosphere was deceiving. The story is told of a newcomer who fancied he ran the risk of drowning when he attempted to cross a little thread of water that lay in his path on the plains of Colorado. However that may be, the mine seemed to be much nearer to us than it really was. Here Fred began to groan and said he had cramps. He threw himself at full length on the snow and fairly screamed with pain. I rubbed him and gave him some relief. He was so exhausted that on the way down the mountain I had to shoulder the load and keep far ahead of him. Fasting as I was, how I longed to break off a piece of the frozen snow and cool my burning tongue and parched lips! The crust on the snow was not hard enough to hold me up, so again I picked my way in the old tracks, which the miners had made coming up the mountain; but they were too short on the down trip and particularly distressing for one who was much fatigued. We stopped at intervals to breathe and I coaxed and encouraged Fred to hold out, the Sheridan being near at hand. Thus step by step we plodded along until at last, ready to drop from fatigue, we arrived at the mine.

We telephoned to Telluride that we would be on time for the funeral. Fred took some hot coffee, and we directed our course to Telluride. The horses were good and had sharp shoes, so there was little danger of slipping. I took the lead and did not spare the whip. Along the wall of the mountain, near the Sheridan mill, the trail is very narrow and skirted by a precipice. Unfortunately a burro train was coming up right at this spot. There must have been more than one hundred burros in the pathway. The driver was cursing and swearing, and a Scotch collie kept nipping the heels of the donkeys. How we were to pass, that was the problem. Burros will not leave the road when carrying a load and they move so mechanically and, it may be added, stupidly, that they crowd one into the ditch. Fred cautioned me and he kept on the inside. I did my best to follow him, but the burros pushed my horse over to the edge, and had I not sprung from the saddle, quickly backed the animal to the edge and kept his fore feet well on the road, I should have been the principal, and not the witness, of a funeral. We escaped serious accident in the sequel, and came to the little valley in which is situated the city of Telluride.

Again Fred was seized with the cramps. I was obliged to help him out of the saddle and lay him on the roadside. After hard rubbing I enabled him to rise and take to the saddle. At that time there was no church, Catholic or non-Catholic, there; the courthouse, which was a respectable building, was used for all kinds of meetings, and by everyone. Shows, lectures, dances, revival meetings, church fairs were all held in the temple of justice. I usually said mass at Mrs. Margowski's, but on state occasions I went to the courthouse, and on this occasion the funeral services were performed there, the majority of those present being Cornish men. At that time few Americans could get work in the Sheridan mine, which employed some three hundred men. The Cornish are fine looking fellows, with broad shoulders, of a stocky build and swaggering carriage. They had the reputation of being first-class miners, it may have been because in their native country they had so much experience in this line of occupation. There were hundreds of them in Telluride, where they practically ran the town. Lovers of good cheer, they spent their money freely, and fairly made the town howl during their all-night carousals. They turned out by the hundred for the funeral and the little courthouse was packed. I said mass and preached an appropriate discourse. After mass I took breakfast and by the time the friends of the deceased had taken a last look at the corpse I was ready to repair to the Lone Tree Cemetery, where we left all that was mortal of poor Flannigan.

Returning, I said my office, and after dinner made some parochial visits to the few Catholics in Telluride and informed them that I should say mass next morning at Mrs. Margowski's. Toward evening I paid a visit to Mr. Ferdinand Kramer, a gentleman who is known to the world of literature under the *nom de plume* of "Credo." It is an appropriate designation for an uncompromising Catholic, who is a ripe scholar, hard student and polished writer. The bent of his mind is philosophical, but no subject concerning man and his best interests is strange to Credo. His style of composition is clear, terse and elegant. Besides devoting himself to literary work, he has skilfully edited a weekly newspaper in the south-western country. The *Colorado Catholic* contains regular contributions from the facile pen of Mr. Kramer. A graduate of Cornell University, and by profession a civil engineer, he has surveyed much of the San Juan country, and possessing large interests in one of the great enterprises of San Miguel County, he bids fair to become one of the wealthiest and most useful men in that section. Often before the morning star veiled its face in the light of the sun have I said mass in this gentleman's cabin at San Miguel, and just as often has he approached the sacred table to refresh himself with the bread of angels. Breakfast over, we sat together talking on literary or religious subjects, while awaiting the sound of the Dallas-bound stage.

Next morning the few Catholics of the town were promptly at hand and many of them received the blessed sacrament of the Eucharist. About nine Fred Thornton, who had slept most of the time since his arrival at Telluride, was up and ready for the home trip. We took our mounts and started for the Sheridan mine, upon reaching which our programme was to turn our horses back, walk up to the top of the range and then down to Porter's, where the other horses had been left the previous day. We arrived at the top of the range by one o'clock and ate the sandwiches which the thoughtful Mrs. Margowski had put into our grip to help us on the way. We came to Porter's in good time and, mounting our horses, rode down the mountain to Ouray, which we reached early in the evening.

As the reader may like to know something more of the companion of my trip, I shall add a few words about him. The following spring he went with his partner to work on some claims which they jointly owned. It was about midsummer, and I happened to be at Silverton, having gone thither the previous Saturday for the Sunday service. In the afternoon of that day I received word by telephone that Fred Thornton was dying of heart disease, and that I must make all haste to Ouray. I had just then one of the best bronchos in that country. The horse was Jack McMahon's and as I was thinking of buying him, the owner let me have him on trial. But he had a chronic saddle-sore on his back, which broke out from time to time, thus rendering him of little value to one who was in the saddle three days of the week. For all that Bill was a first-class stepper; he could trot, pace or run. I rode the animal from Rico in eight hours, stopping an hour at Ophir, and crossing two ranges of mountains. I had a heavy saddle, my vestments and overcoat. It was equal to a seventy-five mile ride on the level road. I let the horse go slowly for a time, until he got warmed up, then I gave him a free rein, and he made Red Mountain in fifty minutes and Ouray in forty-five more. Warm and tired, the animal was full of go still, and I was forced to pull hard on the reins from Red Mountain to Ouray. My arms were tired and the horse's mouth was bleeding from his constant champing on the bit.

I found Fred sitting up in the chair, but after a glance at him saw he was going rapidly. The blood in his face was congested, his lips were growing purple, and he began to exhibit signs of drowsiness. He raised his eyes, put out his cold hand and grasped mine, saying: "Father, you came in a hurry." I said, "Yes, Fred, I was bound to be here in time, if I had to come on the saddle without a horse." Fred smiled and said, "I am not long for this world, I believe I shall never see another sunrise." I could offer no word of encouragement to the dying man, so I told him to prepare for death and I administered to him the last rites of the church. The sisters repeated the prayers for the dying and in the hush of the midnight, his soul winged its flight to the better land. His body, with that of many others, lies mouldering in Ouray's cemetery, awaiting the final resurrection, when there will be no more break-neck rides or death-dealing snow-slides.

FOURTH SKETCH

FROM time to time I went into the mountains and held religious services at some cabin which was a centre of resort for the neighborhood. Here, on the long winter evenings, as well as Sundays, the people gathered,—the young to become acquainted with one another, and the old to exercise their ingenuity in arranging matches for their children and friends. The sagacious dame kept a watchful eye for the young man of steady habits, who chanced to possess the fee of a large, well-stocked ranch. Such an eligible catch won favor with the eager matron whose subtle strokes of diplomacy began with the regulation courtesy, the softest chair in the room and a pressing invitation to tea. It put one in mind of the old-fashioned quilting or corn-husking bee of half a century ago, to observe the lady's strategy, and it would take such keen students of manners and customs as were the writers of the *Spectator* fitly to describe the delicate manœuvres of the wary mother.

In my parish, there were several of those centres where I used to say mass, teach the children Christian doctrine and, upon occasion, administer the sacraments, and not one of them was more attractive than that of Sim Noel, whose name tells his French descent. He lived on the top of the Divide between Dallas and Placerville, where, at an elevation of about 10,000 feet, he owned a ranch of five or six hundred acres. His log cabin stood close to the stage road, in the shelter of a little hill, and a stream of spring water softly murmured at the door-step, inviting

THE DALLAS DIVIDE, MT. SNEFFLES TO THE LEFT

A SOCIAL AND RELIGIOUS CENTER

the passing cavalier to stop and let his broncho drink from the overflowing trough that was considerately set there. If he was given to sociability he spent a few moments in small talk with such members of the family as were engaged in out-door occupations. Sim kept what might be called a road-house and the ladies were skilled in preparing a good meal for the wayfarer,—fresh milk, fresh eggs and fresh veal with rare vegetables from the root house, fresh at any season of the year—making the wayside inn a delectable place of refreshment for the most exacting traveler. In the summer the trout forced their way up the stream to the very door, and when crisped on the pan, constituted a palatable tidbit for the epicure. That Sim had cosmopolitan tendencies may be inferred from the circumstance that one of his sons-in-law was an Irishman, another a Frenchman and a third an American; and that his ways were progressive, appeared from the fact that some of the girls of his family were expert rifle shots, standing in the front rank of the Ouray Rifle Club.

A few miles from this place, and to the southeast, old Sneffles, with his flossy locks of purest white, stood grand, placid and serene as the summer sea in the sunlight. To the south, thousands of acres of fertile land stretched away, with pines of ample girth so distributed as to offer pleasing retreats for camping out. At this altitude it is unnecessary to irrigate the soil, the rainfall in the spring and the summer being copious, and wheat, oats, potatoes, timothy, with a variety of vegetables, are produced in great abundance. This favored region is a paradise for stock in summer and autumn. Through the

IN THE SAN JUAN

openings of pine and spruce on the plateau, the grass in some places grows two feet high. The luxuriant vegetation, the different kinds of grasses, the flowers, the climbing vines, the rich soil, remind one of the tropics, but, the period of growth being very short, cereals, vegetables and fruits indigenous to the altitude, mature quickly. A warm night is as strange as snow in the Sahara desert, so you may rest comfortable under a pair of blankets the hottest night. To the east, this lofty tableland falls in undulating slopes to the valley of the Dallas. A stream of the same name, rising in the dense timber at the foot of Mount Sneffles on the north, drains the lowlands, forms a junction with the Uncompaghre and flowing on to Montrose, swells the volume of the river Grand. To the west, the land declines gently to the canon of the San Miguel, where, far below, the river San Miguel, with musical cadence, rushes on to join the waters that flow into the Pacific. To the south, at a distance of nine or ten miles Tellurideward, the country is rough, hilly, and not well adapted for cultivation, but there are many well-tilled valleys, and the adjoining hills provide a rich supply of fuel and grass. It was in this charming vicinity that now and then I pitched my tent, attended to the spiritual wants of the scattered flock, and enjoyed Sim Noel's hospitality. It was in summer an agreeable place to spend a few days, but the cold in winter is so severe as to leave aching memories of the season.

One summer Father S—k, of Chicago, came to Ouray. He was in search of mineral specimens, flowers, bugs, or any natural curiosities that might promote the study of science. Al-

A SOCIAL AND RELIGIOUS CENTER

though a man of sixty-eight years, he braved the great altitudes and dense woods of southwestern Colorado with all the alacrity of a young man, and he lost no opportunity of ministering to the religious needs of the Slavs and Scandinavians in the mountains. Distinguished as a professor, scientist and polyglot, he was a zealous missionary, worthy of the days of the apostles. Chicago, notably St. Ignatius' College in that city owes no small debt of gratitude to the reverend scientist for the magnificent collection of minerals, flora and insects which he made on his mountain trips. Upon mentioning the purpose of his visit I suggested an outing in the region I have tried to describe. Father S—k was pleased and grateful for the offer. I furnished the tent and horses, and we took with us rations for three days. I had a big black horse which had the habit of balking. He was also somewhat foundered, and shied from time to time on mountain roads. Once I had a rather droll misadventure, while riding this animal under some trees. All of a sudden he sprang aside and left me, like Absalom, hanging to a branch, not by the hair, but by the hands. For the capricious animal I paid the snug sum of eighty dollars, and, upon the recommendation of a Christian gentleman. I pause a moment to remark, "What fools we mortals be!" So, one glorious morning, about the first of September, Father S—k, Father L—n,—a friend of no mean avoirdupois, who was staying with me,—Bobby Burns, the cook, and myself set out on our expedition in the interests of religion and science. We thought at first that Sim Noel's place would be a convenient headquarters for our campaign, but on reconsidering the matter, unanimously agreed that the proper thing was to camp out. We had our coats, blankets and guns,—in a word, a commissariat, fit for a descent on Cuba. The first fifteen miles of the journey we covered without an accident and arrived at the little town of Ridgeway, which lies at the junction of the Rio Grande Southern and the Ouray branch from Montrose. The town enjoyed stirring times while the railroad was in process of construction to Telluride, but when the latter was completed, the depreciation in the value of silver made money scarce and Ridgeway dull. There were few Catholics in the place, but for all that we erected a neat little church. I may say here that I put in some days of as hard work on that little edifice, as well as on one at the neighboring town of Ironton, as I ever did on Iowa's broad prairies, standing before the canvas of a Marsh harvester or beating out the share of a breaking-plow.

As you skirt the foot hills a mile out from Ridgeway, the road takes a sharp turn into the mountains and the ascent is quite precipitous. I had a pretty good load on the express wagon, the horse hitched up with the black was light but gritty, and I took a run at the hill. Just as I got within a few feet of the top the black horse took it into his head to balk, stopped and began to back down. I whipped, the horse kicked and the reverend Fathers shouted and besought me to let them out; but I would not accede to their wishes and they were afraid to jump, as one was old and the other a heavy-weight. The horse kept letting the wagon down, and I had great trouble to keep the road without tipping over.

A SOCIAL AND RELIGIOUS CENTER

At last I allowed my companions to alight, and procuring a stout stick, made the refractory black go up the hill on the jump. It was two in the afternoon when we chose a camping ground, expecting to move on later in the day. Having fed the horses and taken our lunch, with rifle in hand I strolled forth in search of a deer, while Father L—n took a shotgun and Sam, the Irish setter, and went gunning for grouse. Father S—k was turning over logs, looking for bugs, and Bobby Burns was making preparations to dine the clergy in the evening. Plunging into the dense growth of pines I advanced far down the slope for an hour or more, until the sun warned me that it was time to retrace my steps; so I swung around in a half circle, expecting to make camp before dark. Suddenly I heard two or three deer rushing through the woods at a high rate of speed, but I could see none. I thought of the bears which were quite numerous in the dark glens and thick underbrush, but I must confess I had no desire to meet them just then.

Bears are still numerous in some parts of Colorado and a person has a feeling of loneliness, if not dread, when in the thick timber, deep canons, or on the lonely trails most likely to be frequented by those savage animals. Several years ago a miner going over the trail between Rico and Durango had an encounter with a bear, which deserves mention in these sketches. The miner was unarmed and pursuing his way over the short cuts and trails which lead hither and thither from the main road. He had not even so much as a jackknife or a good stick with which he might defend himself. Leaving the main road to shorten his way, he plunged down the gulches over the wooded hills and through the dense copse of underbrush, following a cattle path or deer trail. Coming to one of those scrub-oak hills he found himself in a small park in the midst of the thicket. What was his horror on looking around, when he beheld a large cinnamon bear! There she stood with her two cubs. For a moment the man was seized with fright and before he could realize his situation, she turned and, rising on her hind feet, came toward him with open jaws and outstretched paws. There was no opportunity to run, for she began the fight at once. He was a powerfully built man but had only muscle and a thinly clad body to oppose claws four or five inches long and teeth which could easily crush the arm of a giant. For a few moments the miner parried the blows as best he could, but always with the loss of a part of his clothing, which was torn away by the long claws of the bear. Finally, having lacerated his arms and breast, with one fell stroke she opened his scalp to the back of his neck, knocking him down and placing her huge paws on his breast ready to devour him. Instinctively she turned to look for her cubs and as they were not in sight, left her bleeding victim and hastened in the direction they had taken. The miner fainted. How long he lay there he knew not. At last he came to, and to his horror heard the bear crushing through the brush at no great distance. Gathering his remaining strength and staggering from his great loss of blood, he dragged himself to his feet and fled along the trail with all the haste he could make. He at length reached a farm house and was taken at once to Durango, where the physician sewed up his torn scalp and body. After many months he got well and still lives.

The next morning four stalwart hunters left Durango to visit Mrs. Bruin. They had scarcely entered her dominions when they espied her on a little hillside; she, too, was on the alert and saw them. Without a moment's hesitation she came down to meet them. The cubs followed her, but, mother-like, she turned round and pushed them back with her nose. One of the cubs still persevered in coming, and going back she struck him on the head with her open paw and sent him back up the hill howling. The hunters waited until she got within fifty yards and then poured into her big body a deadly volley which laid her low. The cubs were treated in the same manner as their mother and the boys returned to town proud of their trophies.

Meanwhile the darkness was closing around me, and I found I was lost. Deer trails and cattle trails crossed and recrossed one another, so that I could not take my bearings. After groping to and fro in a place that, to my disturbed fancy, seemed not unlike the fathomless abyss of Schiller's Diver, I was delighted when I came to a little opening, and, standing upon a high rock, fired off my rifle three times at intervals of about three minutes and waited for an answer. After the third report I caught to the left, and in the opposite direction from which I had been moving, the dull sound of a shotgun; and in a few minutes was in camp. Bobby was not there and my two clerical friends had retired for the night, each having chosen a pine tree as a back stop. This novel kind of couch they adopted as no tent had been put up. The fire was burning low and I replenished it so that I might have some warm supper. Having refreshed the inner man I turned in, or rather out, and wrapped in my ulster and blanket, supported my back against a tree. I tried to sleep, but sleep under such circumstances was not easy. The night turned bitterly cold and every little while I arose, dragged a few logs to the fire, and cheered up my companions with the blaze, which, owing to their remote position under the trees, imparted to them more light than warmth. Father S—k complained of having chills, and Father L—n could stand the cold no longer, so I got up once more and found everything covered with a thick hoar frost. Upon inspecting the contents of the wagon I discovered some more clothes, which I distributed among my companions and piled more wood on the fire. I decanted into a little pail some wine which we had taken for an emergency and placed the pail on the fire. It did not take long to boil, and pouring out a liberal dose of the medicine into a tin cup, I approached Father S—k, who was in a shivering condition, and at the point of a gun commanded him to drink it down. Father L—n was obliged to submit to the same imperious treatment, and then the medicine man bethought himself that he, too, was on the point of a chill. It is needless to say that we all felt better for the seasonable decoction; but sleep for the night had fled from our eyes, and we sat around the fire, while Father S—k indulged in long and diverting accounts of his scientific explorations.

With the dawn Bobby appeared on the scene and proceeded to get breakfast. He explained his absence by saying that he had gone to a logging camp a mile away, and finding good quar-

A SOCIAL AND RELIGIOUS CENTER

ters there, remained over night. After breakfast we resolved to decamp. We could not find Father L—n's Sunday coat, a fine broadcloth, and looked everything over and over, but to no purpose. We concluded that it had been lost the previous day; so, jumping on one of the horses, I rode back a distance of three miles to the main road, but found no coat. The Fathers had in the meantime searched the camp again and again, and when they beheld me on my return empty handed, they seemed to be quite disappointed. I drew in my horse, and facing them cried out, "No coat"; just then I noticed that Father S—k looked quite bulky and I inquired, "Father, how many coats have you on?" "Of course only my own," he replied. I sprang from the horse and going up to him discovered to my surprise that he was wearing three coats, one of which, upon examination, proved to be the Sunday broadcloth. We were all well pleased and had a good laugh at Father S—k. Having cleared up the camp, we departed on the journey home and reached Ouray that evening, deerless, grouseless, but not *bug*less, for Father S—k carried back with him a fair supply of beetles and also some mineral specimens.

A few weeks after our excursion I received a sick call to the head of Turkey Creek, which is all of fifty-five miles from Ouray. The message came in the early evening, and I set out on horseback with the messenger. Long before we reached the summit of the divide, darkness had set in, and as we approached Sim Noel's a north wind, accompanied by a drenching rain, swept over the treeless hills that embrace the creek. The lightning played on the hills and sent through the low drifting clouds intermittent flashes of brightness which illumined the inky darkness of our way. From Noel's to Placerville the road is down hill for fourteen miles. The rain came down with full force, and in some places the horses could scarcely keep their feet. Our progress therefore was slow, and it must have been after eleven o'clock when we reached Placerville. We remained at the hotel for an hour, fed our horses and then resumed our journey up the Miguel to the mouth of Turkey Creek. The rain was still falling, but not so heavily as to make it uncomfortable in the saddle. The clouds were breaking and drifting in leaden banks, and now and then showers beat into our faces. The wagon road up the creek is a miserable affair, and at that time it was washed out and cut up by the rain of the past month. Our jaded beasts were permitted to have their own way, so for fully eight miles we advanced very slowly. Time and again the horses, unable to proceed, stood and panted. About two in the morning the rain began to come down again in torrents. Fortunately being near an old mining camp at the head of the creek, where there was a village of empty houses, we dismounted and led our horses into one of the vacant dwellings. Our mackintoshes had kept us dry and excepting our knees, we were in fairly good trim. Lying down in a corner of the cabin we went to sleep, exhausted from our long ride, and when we woke it was broad daylight. We led out our horses and let them eat of the long grass which grew there, and then mounting, we hastened to the sick man. The head of Turkey Creek meant, I ascertained, a vast area of country, for it was noon when we drew up at a cabin not far from the

A SOCIAL AND RELIGIOUS CENTER

Unaweep. The country which we had traversed was new to me and my wonder was excited at the rich soil, heavy grasses and bountiful supply of streams and timber which characterized it. Deer were very plentiful and many coveys of grouse were visible on the trail.

We found the sick man in an advanced stage of consumption and after a series of fresh hemorrhages; but although in his last moments, he was cheerful and happy. He had come from New York to the west; and to regain his health, plunged into the very depths of the pine forest, the odorous balsam of which is beneficial to those who have weak lungs. But he came too late, as was evident from his emaciated condition, and he had but a short time on earth. His ardent desire was to live long enough to return east and see his mother. He spoke of death and the hereafter with a loftier cheerfulness and calmness than Plato's master, and while lamenting the separation from his mother, which he knew was near at hand, he prayed earnestly that his Heavenly Father would grant him the happiness of seeing her once more. After my arrival he grew rapidly better and became even more animated, which was no doubt due to the grace of the last sacraments of the church. The young man had every comfort which money could procure,—a servant to wait on him, a choice assortment of books, musical instruments and even a kodak. The servant man was a queer customer. His master called him "Shinny," and the nickname may have found some authority for its use in the singular character of the man; but he was faithful and thoughtful for the invalid, for whom he considered nothing too good. From the brook, which was close by the cabin, he caught the trout which he cooked with good taste; he scoured the woods for young grouse and sought far and wide everything that was likely to give an appetite to the sick man. In his search for game his daily companion was a hairless Mexican dog, whose bare state caused the burros to lift up their philosophical winkers in admiration. On one occasion Shinny tracked a deer and followed him over a ridge through the thick oak brush, but of course the fleet animal got away from the unsophisticated hunter, and the sportsman returned home, disgusted. But he acquired some experience, for that night he tossed and scratched continually. In the morning he found himself covered with wood-ticks; it was a case where the biter gets bitten, and indeed it is no easy task to get rid of those little insects that burrow deep into the flesh. Shinny's speech had the cockney peculiarity, as he never sounded, not the *h*, but the *r*, in his words when it was proper to do so, as he himself said he was a gentleman from Boston, and presumably, therefore, a person of culture. He also possessed the not uncommon ability of talking on a subject of which he knew little if anything, and his bump of curiosity was so well developed that it did not take him long to learn something of the history of everyone he met. In the pursuit of knowledge, however, like persons of his prying quality, he sometimes encountered laughable rebuffs. His master told me that a stranger who rode on the train between Kansas City and Durango, with Shinny and himself, got even with the former, who had his eyes and ears open all along the route and was swallowing in everything he heard and saw. Having

A SOCIAL AND RELIGIOUS CENTER

been bred in a great city, his ideas of the country and agricultural arts were like Horace Greeley's knowledge of farming. While passing through the prairies he saw many stacks of wheat, of which he knew nothing, so he applied for information to the stranger. He was to the soil born and dilating on the subject of wheat raising, explained minutely everything connected with it, from the time the seed went into the ground until the consumer bought the loaf of bread. The gentleman also descanted upon oats, barley, potatoes, in fact everything that grew, to the child-like delight of Shinny, who, when the train reached Durango, saw a big Navajo Indian standing on the platform. This was a revelation to him. The strange being was arrayed in a calico dress of many colors, his shirt waist was trimmed in beads and shells, his hair in a knot of braid fell over his shoulders, and his trousers had various stripes, while on his head rested a large Mexican hat with a leather strap for a band, and flung in a careless manner over his left shoulder was a beautiful blanket. He was talking to a white man and was greatly worked up over something. Shinny was all on fire to know who he was, so although his obliging companion was helping the sick man with his baggage, the man from Boston could not restrain his curiosity, but running up cried out, "Tell me, sir, who is that? What countryman is he? Where does he come from?" The stockman turned quickly around and replied: "I should judge from his general get up and all he has to say, that he is a gentleman from Boston." The crest-fallen Shinny had no more to say that day. I remained with the sick man until ten o'clock the next day and then went by West Dolores to Rico, where I said mass the following Sunday. I organized a committee of Catholics and took suitable steps for the construction of a church, which materialized under the supervision of my successors.

Next day I started from Rico to Ouray by way of Trout Lake, which is a romantic sheet of water. Nestled in the bosom of mountains of solid rock, it teems with mountain trout, and is an ideal spot for the fisherman who has not the patience to sit on a log for hours and wait for a bite. It is also the source of the power used in some of the adjacent mines. Not many miles to the west is the famous Mount Wilson, the shining guide to many a lone traveler on the mountain trail.

Following the old trail, which worms its way from Trout Lake to Ophir, I came out in a little canon, at the head of which is Ophir camp. A stream of clear water, which forms a junction with the San Miguel a short distance below, rushes along at a rapid rate. At this point the spectator beholds one of the grandest feats of engineering in the state on the Rio Grande Southern. To the ordinary layman, the impossible would confront him in the construction of this aerial line of travel. Like a serpent, wriggling along these mighty walls of granite, or stealing cautiously over a trestle work far above the ground, the iron horse may be seen day after day making its way to Ridgeway to deliver mineral and passengers on the way to Denver and the east. A short distance higher up the town of Ophir is situated, rich in auriferous ores, and containing some of the most valuable mines in the whole country.

A SOCIAL AND RELIGIOUS CENTER

Time and money will make this forgotten camp one of the best in the southwest. A hotel and livery stable, with a few neat cottages dotting the hillsides around, constitute the town. Here I took dinner, rested my broncho for an hour, and speeding homeward, jumped from the saddle in Ouray that evening, after a journey of over fifty miles.

The following November I received from the mother of the young man of whom I have spoken a letter thanking me, at the request of her son, for the little acts of kindness I had shown him, and informing me that two weeks before he had passed to the great beyond. Perhaps she retained in her service the faithful Shinny to lighten the burden it pleased God to put upon her, and that he recounts to her in his own chatty way the many strange things which he saw and heard in the land of mountains and plains.

FIFTH SKETCH

WE had a literary society during the winter months in Ouray. The society was small; so much the better, perhaps, for individuality of character is often lost in big societies, but the few members who were seriously given to self-improvement have attained distinction. The aim of the association was practical, and questions—moral, social and economical—occasioned lively debate. While the speculative was not ignored, the main purpose was to teach how to do the right thing at the right time, and educate the members to be useful. The proceedings of the meetings, which were held once a week, were orderly, and little time was spent on the minutes of the previous meetings or personal explanations, or wasted in mere rhetorical display. It was in a word a school of sense, not of show.

At that time the Irish Land League under the eminent but ill-starred Parnell engaged the attention of Europe and America. I had been more or less identified with the Irish cause from a boy, and was deeply interested in the plans that were devised by intelligent and patriotic sons of Ireland to procure home rule, national independence and, consequently, prosperity for the land of my ancestors. To prove my sympathy with the aspirations of the home-rulers, I occasionally delivered a lecture relating to that subject; sometimes I spoke on other topics which pleased my fancy, while promoting the well-being of our association.

The members of the society prepared for a grand celebration of Patrick's Day, and one of

CELEBRATION OF A FESTIVAL

the features of the commemoration was a lecture which I was to give on the land question in Ireland. There was to be a play, too, and many beautiful recitations, ranging from Shamus O'Brien to Erin's Flag, were designed to add variety and enthusiasm to the entertainment. In March the snow is abundant in the San Juan, and during this special month of Boreas some of the fiercest storms and most destructive snowslides visit this region. For Ireland's national feast great preparations were under way, and the expectation was that the festivities would attract large numbers. The evening of the sixteenth the sun went down behind hoary Sneffles in dark, heavy clouds, which boded no good for Patrick's Day in the morning. By midnight the snow was falling gently and the weather indications were that a great storm was impending. About 2:30 in the morning the door-bell rang violently, and going to the door I learned that there was an urgent sick call for me from Silverton. The messenger had left Silverton the previous night at ten o'clock and driven a team hitched to a sleigh over the range. There was very little danger then, but with this new storm fast approaching, the fresh snow would slide over the hard surface of the old and bear destruction in its path. I enquired who was sick, and when the reply came I knew that the doom of the sick man was sealed, for he had been a hard and constant drinker, and now pneumonia had a firm hold of him. It was the opinion of his friends that he was dying, and he called for the priest, desiring to receive the last sacraments of the church.

The sick man was young, bright, clever, a

hustler and money-maker. When I became acquainted with him he was recovering from one of those periodical sprees which blast life and bring so many to an early grave. He was married, and his wife was a convert to Catholicity. She was one of those confiding creatures, whose heart and soul find in holy church and her consoling doctrines the peace which the world cannot give. But he was of the class, unhappily too large, who, fascinated by the fashion of the world, cast to the winds the practices of religion and outrun the most abandoned in the race of sensuality. Strong drink, evil companions, membership in societies condemned by the church, neglect of the duties which make the true man, wrought his ruin. After a vain effort to reform her dissipated husband, extending over a period of three years, his patient wife was obliged to leave him and seek safety with her parents. I will not dwell upon the harrowing story of a broken heart, but leave to the judgment record of the last day the revelation which I refrain from making

The messenger told me that, as his horses were tired, he must let them rest until six o'clock, when we should set out for Silverton. I slept no more that night, and I was satisfied that I could not deliver my promised lecture that evening. I got up at five, said mass, and requested a brother priest who was my visitor, to excuse me to the audience in the evening and make a short address for me. At six o'clock sharp, we were in readiness to start for Silverton, a terrific drive for one team with a heavy sleigh and a badly drifted road. At Bear Creek Falls, the toll gatherer, who had been there for years, came out to take our tickets, and warned us that we ran the risk of being lost in a slide or in the blinding storm which was advancing apace. At any moment we might plunge over a precipice on the narrow mountain pass. My companion would not turn back, as living in Ouray and boarding a team were expensive, so, despite the difficulties of the situation, he preferred to make Silverton. I was just as anxious to attend the poor fellow who awaited my coming. Accordingly, we continued on our way. Bear Creek Falls was fringed from top to bottom with a delicate embroidery of snow which clung to bridge and rock and shrub, mantling the mountain sides for hundreds of feet down. It is one of the most beautiful water-falls in Colorado. We hastened on our journey without getting out of the sleigh, until we came within half a mile of the second bridge, where we were compelled to alight and shovel snow. The spot is one of tragic memories. The preceding fall Ashenfelter lost a team, wagon and a load of merchandise at this place. Coming up a little rise in the road the collar choked one of his horses, which fell, dragging the other horse toward and over the precipice. The driver saved himself in the nick of time by jumping from the wagon in the direction of the wall; but the outfit went down 2,000 feet. A few hundred yards further on, in the bottom of the creek, lay two dead horses, their necks broken in the mad plunge. There were some other dangerous places in the road, where we might be caught in slides. Coming to the first of these spots, we were pleased to find that the snow had not come down, and that it was not very deep on the incline. About a year before I had been nearly caught right here; moreover, large chunks were breaking loose above and gathering in volume as they rolled down, so I became rather nervous. As I sat in the saddle viewing these suspicious advance guards, a great mass became detached above, and like a flash carried everything before it. It was a close call. When we came to Mother Cline—strange name indeed for a snowslide—we found the passage safe. I thought for a moment of Mother Cary's chickens as applied by sailors to the sea birds, which come on board ships and are the sure harbingers of a storm; but I hoped that the association of ideas, connected with the name Mother Cline, would have no significance for us. This famous snowslide had come down some time before and bore everything away in its track, recoiling from the bottom of the gulch and breaking off the trees on the mountain side for 200 feet. The snow was from sixty to seventy feet deep on the road-bed and in the gulch, and the mass of wrecked matter was a conglomeration of broken trees and huge boulders, some of which weighed from two to three tons. As long as the weather was cold a team could readily cross on the top of the slide, but when the snow melted the county was obliged to cut a tunnel, which was one of the wonders of the Ouray toll road that summer. It was 580 feet long, and high enough for the Concord stage with its six horses to pass through. By late fall the roof was thawed out, but some of the walls remained standing for two years. On our arrival at Ironton we permitted the horses to take a short rest, and meanwhile called on Paddy Commins to ascertain the state of the flock, after

THE SNOW TUNNEL ON OURAY ROAD

CELEBRATION OF A FESTIVAL

which we proceeded to Red Mountain. As we approached the greater altitude the storm almost blinded us, and it was difficult to keep the road. Above the Yankee Girl mine we met a sleigh coming from Silverton, and the men who were in it informed us that the sick man was dead. I at once changed sleighs and started back for Ouray. We stopped at Ironton for dinner at Paddy Commins.' Paddy was a character in his way, and a zealous coadjutor of mine in my missionary labors. He was a grown man at that period, which constitutes an epoch in Irish history, viz.: the night of the Big Wind, and passed through the famine barely with his life. Many a time he spoke of the distress and hardship of those trying days, when men ate grass on the roadside and gaunt starvation stalked through the land. Tired of working at starvation wages on the public works that had been started by an alien government for the relief of the starving Irish, Paddy crossed the British Channel, and for forty years in England carried the hod. On the death of his wife he came to this country, and at the age of eighty, when I got acquainted with him, he was able to do a better day's work than many young men in the full flush of health. He took pride in telling the boys that when he came to Ironton the only apparel he had in the world was a suit of soldier's clothes. He was a strict temperance man, and would not allow a drop of liquor to be brought into his cabin. In the course of his travels he had acquired the knowledge of the cobbler's art, and could repair the men's boots and shoes to the queen's taste. He owned two handsome little houses, which he rented at a good figure, and I have no doubt he had more than one double eagle stored away in the traditional stocking. When the boys chaffed or worsted him in argument he would close the debate by saying: "Give me no more of your after clap." Paddy was deeply attached to his church, which he had grace enough to love more than anything earthly, and he had far more of the ecclesiastical spirit than many great scholars. He took a lively concern in every project that looked to the spread of religion, and gave a helping hand to every good work. Many a hungry man found a substantial meal in the patriarch's cabin. He was sexton and general utility man in the little parish at Ironton, where, in my absence, he watched over the flock and kept a record of whatever it was useful for me to know. He still lives, a fine specimen of an honest old man.

After dining at Paddy's, and wishing him many happy years and many returns of Patrick's Day in the morning, the day he was born in the land beyond the sea, I set out for Ouray in one of the most desperate storms of snow and wind I ever faced. I have been caught in a blizzard in all its prairie tantrums and stood it for ten hours at a time, when the cold was so bitter as almost to freeze a man to death, but I never experienced a storm which for severity and fierceness equaled that mountain maelstrom of the canon. There was not a sense that did not have its appropriate scourge in that furious cyclone or whirlwind; and so thick and dense was the snow that it was impossible at times for the horses to move. We got out of the sleighs, waded hip deep through the soft snow and felt for the road in broad daylight, creeping along the wall to be certain that

CELEBRATION OF A FESTIVAL

we were not rushing headlong into the precipice. After four hours of stumbling, falling in the snow and digging a way for the horses, and when we had almost given up the hope of ever coming out alive, we appeared in Ouray at five in the evening and celebrated Patrick's Day, or rather night, as it had never before been celebrated. There was a large audience awaiting the big programme, and the skillful performance of the play, which represented Ouray's best histrionic and musical talent, compensated for any shortcomings in the lecture of the wornout traveler. The play was Sheridan's masterpiece, "'The School for Scandal,'' and relieved the tragic character of the lecture by its light, comic vein. It was strange to see such a play, and one with such a name, rendered far up in nature's mountain theatre. It is sufficient to say that the whole entertainment was received with enthusiastic favor, and that it was a genuine Patrick's Day celebration. Let the Irishman be ever so far away, when Patrick's Day arrives, his heart, untrammeled, returns to the home of the venerable Granuaile and the memories associated with Ireland's patron saint, concerning whose work the following quaint ballad was composed, perhaps, by one of the ancient bards, and translated by some Irish scholar:

Ye offspring of Seth of the ancient belief,
Old Granu's true sons by adoption,
These lines most sincere I commit to your care
For perusal and also instruction,
Concerning that great and apostolic man,
The glorious St. Patrick, you shall understand,
Who banished idolatry out of our land,
Made Erin to blaze with true zeal and devotion,
He left us the happiest isle in the ocean,
And Patrick's Day in the morning.

IN THE SAN JUAN

When he came to our shore
Our land was spread o'er
With witchcraft and dark necromancy;
Deluged, the scribe says,
By such gross, evil ways,
As was pleasing to Beelzebub's fancy.
This champion of Christ did all magic expel,
Those imps of perdition he did them repel,
Their worship he stopped and their idols, they fell.
Our Savior's bless'd name was praised through the nation,
The cross, it was held in profound veneration,
And Erin complied with the sign of salvation,
And Patrick's Day in the morning.
The peer and the peasant, the prince, I declare,
To the font of baptism, they all did repair;
St. Patrick, he freed them from satan's great snare,
He showed them the path that led to Mount Sion,
The manner to live and the way for to die in,
And none would be lost who were patronized by him,
And Patrick's Day in the morning.

Fatigued by great labors and hardships, 'tis true,
And aged one hundred, likewise twenty-two,
On the seventeenth of March he bid them adieu;
His soul took its flight to the mansions of glory,
Where fame still records it in sacred history,
For divesting our island of serpent and Tory.
He left us the happiest spot in the ocean,
And Patrick's Day in the morning.

And, now for to end those few lines I have penned,
Oh! Blessed St. Patrick, remember
How thy people did stand
For thy faith in this land,
Tho' distressed, like the birds in December.
It is now on the verge of the eight hundredth year,
We've supported thy land through troubles and fear,
And stood by the doctrine you planted so dear,
In spite of seduction, oppression or killing,
To this present day we still have five million,
Who are always both active and ready and willing
To aid your just cause in the morning.

While the versification of this ballad may violate the rules of poetical composition, the sentiment is so good that it has been thought not amiss to embalm it in a sketch of a Patrick's Day celebration. It is not unlikely that it is one of the ballads which were more common in Ireland fifty years ago than to-day. It possesses a delicious combination of piety and humor.

That spring, pneumonia was prevalent in the San Juan, and many of the boys crossed the range for the last time. Deaths and funerals became so common that I was brought into frequent communication at the church services with non-Catholics, with the result that some of those who afterwards came to the hospital ill were converted through the kindly admonitions of the never-tiring sisters. Indefatigable workers and wholly devoted to their vocation of sacrifice, they were constantly in the service of their patients, for the spiritual and physical welfare of whom they considered no fatigue great, no vigil long. True sisters of charity, they won the love of all. Many a hardened sinner who might have scorned the advice of even dear friends, hearkened to the counsel of the sisters and at the eleventh hour were reconciled to God; there were not a few who rose reformed from a sick pallet, and to this day thank their gentle nurses for the spiritual and corporal works of mercy which were performed in their behalf. Of this class were two brothers from Missouri, who had been working at the mines. One of them was taken ill and for four or five days struggled between life and death. The sister who was in attendance at his sick bed, seeing that the end was near, spoke to him of the necessity of preparing for the life to come. She told him that he must be baptized if he wished to enter the kingdom of heaven and be instructed in the principal mysteries of religion. The good words of the teacher did not fall on incredulous ears; the young man heard the voice of the spirit and did not harden his heart. The priest came to him and he received the sacraments with edifying dispositions and died a saintly death. His remains were followed to the cemetery by a large number of miners, and his broken-hearted brother, as he stood bareheaded at the foot of the grave, was seized by a congestive chill, which rendered his immediate removal to the hospital imperative. The doctor was summoned at once and pronounced the case pneumonia. The usual remedies were applied, and the sisters did everything in their power to save his life. The first night of his illness, he became delirious and his constant cry was: ''I want to become a Christian; baptize me, for I am dying;'' and when he came to himself the next morning, he continued to express the same desire. I was sent for, and informed him that he must wait until he was instructed, and that as soon as he got well I would give him the requisite instruction; but that if he were in serious danger of death I would baptize him at any time. This satisfied him, and during the day he showed signs of improvement, but as evening came he began to sink so rapidly that I baptized him and prepared him for death. As the morning drew near, with the sisters kneeling at his bedside and praying for him, he breathed forth his regenerated soul to his Maker. That morning, while the body of the dead man awaited the arrival of his friends, I went to Grand Junction to assist a neighboring priest. I have often been struck by the wonderful conversions that occur at our hospitals. Men who spend long lives of utter spiritual abandonment are suddenly touched by the merciful hand of God, and the Divine visitation, which they regard as a curse, becomes the greatest blessing. Brought to themselves during the tedious hours of illness, they begin to see the folly of their past life and in the face of suffering, the vision of truth comes to them. They repent and become good Christians, or die well.

SIXTH SKETCH

DURING my last two years at Ouray, and after Silverton and Rico had each a pastor, I now and then took a holiday trip into the mountains. On such occasions, I trailed a deer, gave a wide berth to a bear, or killed grouse, which were fairly plentiful on Cow Creek. The mountain trout, too, were a tempting morsel to the patient disciple of Izaak Walton. The fisherman can always catch enough to eat, and the trout, fried in bacon, make a savory dish. Then the air is so bracing that you have the best of seasoning in a vigorous appetite. These short excursions, though physically exhausting and tiresome in a mountainous country, are an excellent antidote for mental overwork and the parish worries that come, when a church is in debt. Building churches, collecting money and paying debts soon wear a man out.

I had two missions besides Ouray, viz.: Ironton and Ridgeway. Through the active efforts of the generous Catholics of these stations, a neat little church was erected at each town. I always said mass, and had an evening service on Sunday in Ouray, and I alternated the second Sunday mass at Ironton or Ridgeway. For the purpose of attending these missions, I kept a pair of bronchos, roan in color, weighing, perhaps, 800 pounds each, and fast steppers. Leaving Ouray on Sunday morning at about six o'clock, I drove up to Ironton, a distance of nine miles. I let the ponies go at an easy gait, as there was a distance of 2,000 feet to be overcome in the ascent; but, on my return to

Ouray for the 10:30 o'clock mass, I did not let the grass grow under the little fellows' feet. Many a time have I descended the stony road along a mighty wall of granite, with the wheels of the buggy within twenty inches of a precipice, 2,000 feet deep. The journey I could make in the brief space of forty minutes. Now and then some visitor to Ouray would desire to come with me and view the magnificent scenery; but after one experience the curiosity of such a one would be more than gratified. The pace was too rapid, and the situation too thrilling for the greatest sensation lover. I once took a young man to Ironton on Sunday morning, and having been delayed beyond the usual time after mass I let the ponies fairly fly over the road on my way back. My companion clutched the seat of the buckboard and held on with all his might. He screamed and said: "Father, I must have heard something crack." I inquired if the wheels were on and he said yes. "Well, then," said I, "there is no danger," and I cracked the whip again. The little ponies, being light and willing, moved down the mountain at a tearing pace without injury to themselves or passengers.

The broncho is by far the best and fastest saddle horse in the mountains. Not too heavy to climb the highest places, it is light enough to move down the steep incline with ease and security. Nearly as sure-footed as the mule, without its slow gait, the broncho will pick its way with skill over a narrow, stony path on a mountain ridge which is scarcely a foot wide and where the broad-footed horse would destroy himself and rider. The broncho may fall without injury to himself or rider, and once down, the latter is able to bring him to his feet again, turn him around in the trail or dig him out of the snow, something he could not do with a heavy horse. The staying powers of the broncho are of the first quality and no large horse can stand fatigue, hunger, hardship and abuse so well as the despised broncho, which, during the past years, has been sold in the west as low as two dollars and a-half.

It has been said, time and again, that a man on foot can outrun a horse carrying a rider down a steep mountain. This claim was put to test some years ago on that steep and narrow trail which lies between Marshall Basin and Telluride. The endurance, speed and certainty of this animal in keeping his feet, where it was impossible for a man to go down the almost perpendicular cutoffs, while bearing a rider, proved to the satisfaction of all that the broncho was capable of accomplishing leaps down precipices and over craggy points, which even the Rocky Mountain sheep would not dare attempt. Thousands of dollars changed hands on the event to which I allude, as many people came to see this novel contest of four miles down the mountain between horse and man.

The trip to Ridgeway was over twelve miles. After saying mass there on Sunday morning at nine o'clock, and giving a short instruction to the people, I had little time to reach Ouray for the second mass; the ponies, however, stood it well and passed everything on the road. But Sunday was their hardest day, as it was mine.

In the early September of 1890 I planned a hunt to Cow Creek, and took with me a young friend who was not distinguished for his marks-

THRILLING INCIDENTS OF A HUNTING TRIP

manship, his opportunities of using a gun having been few and far between. His name was Dennis, but not the Dennis who is made fun of at the political convention. I also took a young man who was born within the sound of the flowing Rhine, three horses, rifles, shot-guns, and rations for forty-eight hours. We brought our overcoats and a blanket each for a night on the mountain. Dennis, and Van, which was the name of the other member of the party, and a crack shot, intended to kill deer, and myself and my dog Prince were in quest of grouse.

Everyone that has been in Ouray knows where the Horse Shoe is—east of the city. It is a vast amphitheatre, the wall of which rises several thousand feet above the city, indeed, so high that nothing but the bare rocks appear against the eastern sky. When the sun rises over these lead-colored peaks and the rays of his golden light quiver upon nature's towers, the scene is grand and impressive. In winter the hand of the clock points to ten when the sun shows his face, and in the west old Sneffles hides the last ray of the departing monarch by four in the evening. So, the days are short in Ouray's winter. The range on the northeast gradually sinks for twelve miles to the northwest into stunted foot hills, which fade out of sight in the verdant valley of the Dallas. To the northeast of a city, which is thought by many to be the most picturesque in the world, the resident of Ouray may, as he sits in his doorway, easily trace the different periods of geological formation in the red granite walls which, rising thousands of feet, form one of the most beautiful features of a mountain picture in the San Juan. In the summer, when the snow

IN THE SAN JUAN

is melting, a stream of limpid water rushes from the far-away peaks through a small ravine in the mountains above. The ravine is studded with scrubby pines, with here and there the golden willow, the wild plum tree and the swaying aspen, which is at home on the lofty heights. As the rivulet rushes over the cliffs, it falls several hundred feet and tones whatever of the stern may be in the scene.

THE CASCADE OF OURAY.

What murmur breaks the stillness,
Stealing down from yon high walls;
Coming forth from rock and crevice,
Whisp'ring music, as it falls?

'Tis the cascade from the mountains,
Rushing down the craggy way;
Dashing o'er the time-worn boulders
To the valley of Ouray.

Now it sounds far up the mountains,
In a voice that seems to say:
"I am coming forth to gladden
The beauty of Ouray."

Nearer, louder, sounds its music,
As it marches on the way,
Gath'ring up the spring and streamlet,
Leaping down upon Ouray.

High above the city's grandeur,
How its seething volumes play,
Clad in gold and silver sunshine,
Rushing down upon Ouray.

It was our intention to climb this mountain. To do this we had to go down the road from Ouray for about two miles, then turn to the right, go up a gulch, creep along a trail that had special dangers for horses, and come out on Horse Thief

Ouray, Colorado

trail. We were ready to start at four in the morning. Prince was delighted, jumping gayly about and wagging his tail. Our progress at first was slow, Dennis taking the lead, with Van second, and myself bringing up the rear. Climbing a steep grade in the mountains is obviously a hard task, every few yards one must rest, and to urge a horse would be simply to kill him or force him to lie down on the trail. The rider must dismount and lead the horse. Dennis was a miner, so was Van, and it was difficult for me, who weighed 200 pounds, to keep up with them. We crossed little streams and stretches of valleys, well watered, well timbered, and carpeted with the russet leaves of many an autumn and the fossilized remains of deer and mountain sheep. Here was a soil which for richness can scarcely be equaled, and besides there was enough of timber for all uses. It was, perhaps, through such a paradise the Grecian leader passed on the famous retreat of the Ten Thousand, and, as I recall the memory of those pleasing valleys, I regret that I cannot describe them with the pen of the classical writer. While I plodded along, gazing on the virgin forest and the fertile country that would make happy homes for thousands, the thought of the folly of mortals unnumbered who quit the country for the city, came to my mind. "We leave our sweet plains and farms for smoke and noise." All over the world tens of thousands are toiling in dingy shops for the merest pittance, while in Colorado and the great west, acres, nay regions, of arable land summon the industrious to prosperity and happiness. It is true that you cannot raise everything you may want on the high tablelands, but it is just as true that a man's wants are not his needs. All the necessaries of life may be produced—wheat, oats, barley, rye, potatoes and vegetables of all kinds, and wood and water are abundant. More timber has been destroyed in Colorado by forest fires and now lies rotting on the ground than could be put to profit by the inhabitants of the state for a century.

At sunrise we came out on the plateau, far above the mountain, at whose base Ouray hides from the winter's blast. The sun was just stealing over the mountains on Cow Creek, and over that long range far away on the Cimmaron, whose jagged peaks are like a piece of embroidery on the sky in the background. To the west, the Blue Mountains of Utah lie like a coronet on the horizon, for the mists which always seem to hang over these mountains had been scattered by the effulgence of the morning light. From our position we could descry the very spot on which the city of Grand Junction stands, although seventy miles away, and the houses in Montrose could be seen at a distance of thirty miles. The Uncomphagre, a deep blue ribbon of water, winding its way through the valley of the Dallas, imparted to the prospect still more life and beauty. We were almost ravished by the sight. Dennis had no place in his mind for Killarney, her placid lakes and softly sloping hills; Van thought no more of the smoothly flowing waters of the blue Rhine and I could hardly realize the tame and even sweep of Iowa's fruitful farms, while the vision of Colorado's mountain scenery held us enthralled. The grass on the plateau was wet with hoar frost, and here, while preparing our guns, we let the horses eat. We followed Horse

Thief Trail for about two miles, when we came to an opening, or rather a gap in the mountain, peeped down the craggy defile, and to our delight we beheld several deer and a bunch of Rocky Mountain sheep standing on a shelving rock 1,000 yards below. We determined to have some of the deer, for there was a law against shooting sheep, but the game had scented us and were moving down the gulch. We decided to follow them, leading our horses down a most dangerous slope into which the water was seeping out from the mountain. Presently we were up to our knees in the splashing mud, and the horses floundered up to their breasts. After many severe efforts, we came out on a rocky point, bedraggled with mud and with much of the hunting spirit taken out of us; we looked much more like Sherman's bummers than the sportsmen you read of. After examining the ground and perceiving that we could not get down the mountain, our opinion was that it would be no easy task to get back the way we came. We were in a bad trap, and the game was gone. In this awful dilemma we made up our minds to face the difficulty of returning by the way we came. It took two hours to advance 200 yards, and I believe Dennis would bear me out in saying that it was a very perplexing situation.

Having gained the trail once more, we followed it, and in passing through a piece of woodland, were surprised to hear the sharp crack of a rifle at such an early hour, a quarter of a mile to the right. In a few moments, crashing through the brush several hundred yards away, came a magnificent specimen of a buck, with antlers thrown back. He was going, I thought, fifty or sixty miles an hour, and in a twinkle was over the hogback and out of sight. To follow him was out of the question, and we moved on carefully, on the lookout for more deer. We had gone but a short distance when we met a tall country man—afterwards I learned he was a Missourian—carrying a Springfield rifle that may have done good service in the Civil war, as the stock was notched and bruised. He was a typical Yankee, with long legs, a short back, and having that easy shuffle which indicates long acquaintance with frontier life. He wore a slouch hat, and rolled a quid of navy in his jaw as if to moisten his tongue, for he seemed to be warm and perspired freely. "Did you see a wounded buck come up this way?" he broke in, without any formal introduction. "He was on the run down the mountain and I caught him on the hind quarter. I'm certain," said the man, "as he limped after the shot." I was about to say that he was on the run yet, and that he did not limp when he passed us, but we told him that we saw the deer pass at a rapid gait, and that he showed no signs of being disabled. From the man's excitement it was evident that he had the buck fever and had not seen the back sight on his gun when he fired. We moved on over the mountains, while our new acquaintance pursued the trail of the deer, which he hoped would soon lie down and die.

Having crossed a range of mountains, we came to the headwaters of one of the many streams which empty into Cow Creek. This was a lovely spot, with some timber and a deserted cabin. It was just the place to camp. The grazing was excel-

THRILLING INCIDENTS OF A HUNTING TRIP

lent, there was much grass and water, with an abundance of dead wood to make fire and boil our coffee. While selecting a spot and still in our saddles, Van put his hand to his mouth and said: "Hush ! see the deer." We looked over a hillock and about half a mile away, counted fourteen deer in single file, standing on the trail and looking directly at us. Apparently, not disconcerted by our appearance, they began to move along slowly. Van took the rifle and rode down a gulch which was near by, while Dennis went around the mountain on the other side; thus, some one would have a chance of a shot. I remained in camp, and was cautioned not to shoot for an hour and a-half. I dismounted and rested in the shade of the tree, but Prince, with true setter instinct, was nosing around and soon raised a grouse, then another. I was tempted to have a crack at the game, but I kept my promise. I looked for the boys. They had passed out of sight round the mountain; I waited and waited; the sun became hotter, and I caught no ring of the rifles yet. I was afraid to move, lest I should disturb the grouse, and Prince was tied and begging piteously to be freed. At length, making up my mind to wait no longer, I turned the dog loose and the gun, too. In a very short time I had fifteen grouse, and was tired shooting, when the boys, footsore, came into camp, without a deer. We took lunch together and were quietly resting in the shade when our tall Missourian came up with his burro, frying-pan and camping outfit. We invited him to have something to eat, and discussed the probability of getting some deer. He knew of a place, a good place, too—it is a failing with every hunter to know of a place, or course, a good place, but the particular place of the Missourian was ten miles from where we were sitting. He assured us, however, that if we adopted his suggestions and remained over night at his place, we certainly should get a deer. This being the object of our excursion we acquiesced.

In the middle of the afternoon we set out over that barren region, reaching an elevation where there was scarcely a vestige of vegetable life, and keeping along the backbone of the mountain for miles, saw only a few skulking coyotes and foxes. These we would not shoot, lest the nobler game might be put to flight, but notwithstanding this reserve, a deer did not appear the whole afternoon. As the sun was setting, we descended the mountain and found ourselves in a level plain through which a sluggish stream was trying to make its way. This stream we followed up for two miles to its source. Our Missourian friend proposed that we should camp here, as a half mile farther on we should enter the coveted park, in which we were to make our debut at the first streak of dawn. I shall never forget that night. Cold! the ice was nearly half an inch the next morning on the little lake that lay near our camp. On one of the adjacent cliffs we saw a mountain lion, which was too far away for a shot. We selected a spot for the night, picketed our horses and were soon enjoying a hot cup of coffee. We then spread our blankets on the grass, put on our overcoats and turned in for the night. I occupied the mid quarter of our resting-place as far as there could be a middle, for it was four in a bed. I must admit that I had the warmest place, but that is not saying much, as it turned out to be extremely cold. All night the mountain lions and coyotes kept up a mournful howl, and what we supposed was a bear tore through the underbrush. Even the ponies and the burro joined in the dismal concert, which contained so many discords that it was hard to sleep. That we were disturbed by such weird music, and in such desolate surroundings, need not disturb the reader, for brown and cinnamon bear were at one time very numerous in the San Juan and quite a few still remain, affording great pleasure to the true sportsman and filling the fellow who is always hunting bear with great fear. Black bear, of which there are many of the small variety, are not considered of much value in the list of the hunter's scalps. Camping out in the haunts of those animals is not so dangerous as the average novel reader thinks. The bear is a matter of fact animal and generally minds his own business. It will never attack man except when driven by hunger to desperate straits, wounded, or in defense of its young. A very comical story is related of three prospectors who were encamped where there were many cinnamon bears. At night the boys took great care to have a large log on the fire to keep away those prowling monsters who, like all wild animals, fear fire. The smell of bacon as well as the remains of deer brought them very close to the tent at night, and the smashing of twigs by these heavy-weights of the forest kept the miners from sleeping, so that at intervals the latter got up and shot off their rifles, which had the effect of scaring them away. Miners take turns in cooking on those prospecting excursions and all become more or less perfect in the culinary art. One morning when two of them were in bed and the third had gone to the creek for a bucket of water, a large cinnamon bear made a call. The bacon was sizzling on the fire and the coffee making its first effort to boil. The bear stood up on its hind feet, grasped the tent at the opening, pulled it aside and boldly walked in, paused and surveyed the situation. Tom and Bill were in bed—knives, pistols, revolvers and Winchesters were within easy reach. The first sight of the bear put them into a state of utter helplessness. Indeed, it is said that Bill was so frightened that when the bear turned his back for further investigation, he hid under his companion. The bear at once began operations by putting his paw into the frying-pan and seizing a large piece of bacon. But he certainly did not calculate on the fire and dropped the tempting morsel; howling with pain, he danced around the room for some time, during which the boys in the bunk never moved. Seeing a sack of flour on a box he grabbed it in his paws and ripped the sack from one end to the other, scattering the flour in every direction. Looking at his white paws for a moment he thought the color good and lay down and rolled over and over, so that he rose up a polar bear, and scenting the sugar close by in the larder, he pulled out the sack and soon had devoured the greater part of it. In the mean time the third man returned from the creek, and catching a glimpse of the bear climbed a tree and waited until the bear departed, when he came down, and taking a Winchester, followed the trail. He did not have far to go when he saw bruin sunning himself a short distance away on a ledge of rock. A few well-aimed shots did the rest, and the boys had bear meat for some time. Next to the bear, the mountain lion is the largest, most powerful and dangerous wild animal in the mountains. He makes his home in the rugged cliffs, where he finds caves running into the depths of the mountains. From these dens, far away from the farmhouses, he descends into the valleys at night and pounces upon calves, sheep and sometimes full-grown horses and cattle. It is said that lions are natural cowards and never face man except when cornered and forced to fight. The sound of a human voice fills them with fright and they at once flee. I have known the case of a woman still living in the western part of the state who had a thrilling experience with a mountain lion. She went out into the field one day to dig potatoes and brought the baby with her, wrapping it up and leaving it in the wagon close to which she was working. Looking up she was amazed to see what she took for a large dog, jump nimbly into the wagon. Grasping the hoe, she ran toward the wagon, screaming at the top of her voice. The lion went up toward the child, seized it by the clothes and tried to carry it off; this it could not easily do, as the child was heavy and well wrapped in a blanket. As the woman approached the wagon and the dog came running up, the lion fled without making an attempt to fight. But lions are not always cowardly.

To take up, however, the thread of my sketch, I must say that Dennis was his name for that night anyhow, for he had to get up often and keep the fire going. Just as day was breaking, we sallied forth and skirted the mountain side until we came to the edge of the park. It consisted of about 200 acres and the Missourian had not exaggerated its charms. Through it ran a murmuring stream, which flowed far down into Cow Creek. Van went along the mountain to the right, the Missourian to the left, and, armed with a gun loaded with buckshot, I was to wait for the deer at the only outlet we knew of. Dennis had to change the pickets of the horses and then join the party. I took my position behind a clump of thick willows until it was clear day, but no deer was in sight. After a while I meandered down the creek in the direction taken by my companions, who as yet had not fired a shot. Presently they returned and reported that there was not a fresh track in the park and that there were no deer. So we turned loose and soon the grouse were on the move and rifle and shotgun spoke in loud tones in the mountain stillness. By nine o'clock we had bagged quite a number of grouse and all assented to my proposal, that we should go down the stream and through the canon to Cow Creek. Dennis brought the horses, and for a mile or so, we followed the bed of the stream. The water was shallow and clear as crystal; the mountain trout could be seen breasting the stream in the swirling rapids; and on either side the porphyry, granite or quartz walls rose thousands of feet. At length, we came to a cascade over which we could not take the horses. We were compelled to turn back. On the left was a small opening in the wall, which had developed into a good sized gulch, down which trickled a stream, the bed of which was full of huge boulders and dead trees. Up this gulch I headed my horse and called the boys to follow me. The ascent was tiresome, but at last we arrived at the top of a hogback—in the ocean's bed it would be called a reef. It was very narrow, and we had to employ the utmost care to prevent our horses from slipping off. On taking observations, and finding that we were about six miles from where we took lunch the day before at noon, we set out in that direction. Coming down to the base of the mountain, through one of the most perilous passes, as it was the path of a yearly snowslide, landslide and rockslide, we encountered the remains of a burro with the packsaddle still thrown around the bones, drills, hammers, axes, kettles and all the camp utensils necessary for an outfit. A few boards scattered here and there, indicated that a cabin had been swept away in a snowslide.

THE SNOWSLIDE

With rumbling tones, the mountain woke,
Tossed like a giant, shuddered, spoke,
Like peals of thunder in storm's wake,
When leaden clouds the lightnings break.
The calm, placid snow untrodden lay,
Gath'ring in depth from day to day,
Till rock and tree and wooded shade,
Were covered close with frost inlaid,
Gulches are filled and dells unseen.
Lo! nature in her winter scene,
That will remain, unchanged by sun,
Till springtime floods in torrents run,
Which off its side to valleys flow,
And make the peach and apple grow.
The farmer, glad with hopes of gain,
Prepares his crop for grateful rain,
Which, glist'ning bright in banks of snow,
In summer's heats begins to flow,
Waters the plains and arid farms,
And gives to earth her youthful charms.
But, hark, the power on Sneffles crest,
Hurls the huge mass from off its breas

> Wildly adown the slope it speeds,
> The pines it snaps like hollow reeds;
> Boulders and trees dashed out and in,
> It sweeps along with deaf'ning din,
> Catching them up, twisted and broke,
> The relics of a single stroke.
> Far, far below in mountains moat,
> Crushed, buried in the abyssmal throat.
> The fallen tree, the cabin bare,
> Tell the bold miner to beware,
> While seeking wealth on mountain side,
> Death's embrace of the rueful slide.

We looked carefully about for the remains of man, but found none. From the appearances we concluded the accident had happened several years before. At the base of this mountain, we took our rations, which were down to bed rock, and then pushed on over the mountain, coming out at a point about two miles from where we came up the preceding day. Van got his eye on some fresh deer tracks; and, as it was then only about two in the afternoon, we determined to follow these tracks some distance. For about three miles, the deer kept the top of the range, swinging around to the Dallas. They then turned down into the timber, and we all dismounted, tied our horses, and made a bold dash for a deer. While the boys kept in the trail, I went around the side of the hill. In this manner the whole gulch might be more easily covered. Prince was with me, and hard to hold. All at once, the loud report of a Winchester broke the silence, and a moment later a deer rushed up the gulch, tried to jump a high bank, missed it, and fell back, turning completely over; plainly he was a much-scared deer; but, retrieving himself in an instant, he was up and gone. The boys followed the trail down the gulch and were soon lost to view. I hunted for some time, killing half a dozen grouse, and waited patiently for their return. At last I began to think that they were lost. It was almost dark, the trail was very dim, the autumn leaves were falling, and the wind began to whirl them over the road. After firing my gun several times, the boys came back, empty-handed and disgusted with deer hunting.

As night was fast approaching, we mounted and rode away. We got along pretty fairly for a short time, but, as we lost the trail, it was fully a quarter of an hour before we found it, and time was then valuable. We were at an altitude of 11,000 feet with only a deer trail, which ran around the backbone of the range to lead us down, and as long as we kept it, we were safe. But Dennis, as well as the Missourian, thought we should go down one of the many gulches to the left; in their opinion, any one of them would bring us to the main road in the valley. I protested that we could not get through the fallen timber, while, by keeping the ridge, we should arrive sooner at our destination, although the distance was twice as great. My protest was vain, so we went down the gulch. It must have been about six o'clock when we reached this conclusion. As we descended, the timber became thicker and the fallen trees lay in every possible position, forming a network of interlaced pines, poplar and shrubbery. The situation was sufficiently exasperating, but we had to trudge along, carrying our guns and leading our horses. Becoming thirsty, we could find no water, as the gulch was dry. My companions wished to camp, but I was determined at all

IN THE SAN JUAN

hazards to reach Ouray that night. The gulch finally narrowed down to a few feet in width, and the bottom was filled with holes, washed out by the summer's rains. Time and again, we stumbled, and the horses stumbled with us; in fact, it was a series of stumblings over fallen timber, until we came to a great washout, which checked our further progress. Here again the boys said they wanted to camp, but I was inexorable. Burning with thirst and sweating like a harvest hand, I turned up the side of the mountain, leading my horse over the rocks, jumping from shelf to shelf, and feeling my way with my gun where I could not see. Again, I sought the bottom of the gulch, and reached a better path. At last we struck another gulch, which contained a welcome stream. Thankful for this unexpected blessing, we knelt on the brink and drank to our heart's content. After a few moments' rest we resumed our journey and came out on the road. We reached Ouray at three in the morning, after a chapter of surprises and mishaps. Our hunting expedition had proved a failure; and, with the exception of a few grouse, we had nothing to show for two days' hard work. However, we had a splendid outing, for, besides the exciting incidents of the trip, we were delighted with the magnificent scenery of the mountains. While the sublime prevails, the varied elements of the grand and romantic are not wanting. No man can travel through the mountains without a deepening impression of the majesty of the Creator; no one can stand in the presence of the snow-capped peaks, over which sunshine and shadow pursue each other, without feeling an impulse to elevate his soul to

God, the author and the finisher of the beautiful and the sublime. A trip to the mountains convinces the religious mind of the existence of divine power, wisdom and goodness, and inspires the man of good will with the resolution to seek first the kingdom of God and His justice. Where all is so divine, surely the spirit of man should not be merely human.

SEVENTH SKETCH

THE San Juan is inhabited by people of European extraction, as well as descendants of the aborigines. The proud blood of the Aztecs flows in the veins of the Mexican, who urges over the mountains the pack train, loaded down with everything from a quarter of beef to the long slender bar of iron which is used for the mine track. The wiry Scotchman, the robust Irishman work side by side with the stocky Italian and the self-possessed American. Now and then the thrifty Scandinavian finds his way to the camp congress of the nations, and shows himself to be a giant of the drill. The phlegmatic Austrian stands side by side with the stanch son of Cornwall. Here is a variety of nationality and character which promises a wide field for the study of human nature. The natural virtues shine in the lives of these hard-working miners with a splendor that finds its counterpart in some of Rome's greatest men. When sickness, accident, or death comes to the cabin, all thoughts of self are dismissed. But when snowslides come down the mountain side, bearing many to death, when pneumonia afflicts the young and strong, or the premature blast opens the day of eternity to the most careful and virtuous, these disciples of humanitarianism are thrown into a panic. To the religious mind the reflection then comes, that while natural virtues are good enough for passing ends, positive religion based on divine faith is necessary to stem the tide of fear and despair that floods a man's heart when death knocks at the

The Burro Train

A DEVOTED MOTHER IN ADVERSITY

door. This truth vividly struck me when standing at one of those death-bed scenes at which the clergyman is called to assist.

I once met an old man who exemplified many of the qualities of natural, as distinguished from revealed, religion. He was about sixty-five years old when I made his acquaintance. Having served in the Mexican war, and commanded one of Joe Reynolds' steamboats upon the Mississippi, he acquired the title of captain by courtesy. Generous to a fault, and with a hand never closed to the needy, the captain was honored and respected by all who knew him. At sixty-five he was hale and hearty, and as active as a man of forty. The rich strikes attracted him to Colorado, and through his influence, which proved to have been unwisely exerted, many of his friends lost their investments in barren prospects. As to himself, he struggled some years, working the mines alone, and striving to interest others in what he believed would develop into paying properties. He lost his money by degrees and was compelled to lock the door on the tunnel, abandon his little cabin on the hillside and seek the mining camp, where he dragged out a poor existence by keeping a lodging house. Meeting the boys in the street, he would solicit them to patronize his house so that he might make a few dollars to help him along. When I visited the camp I always occupied his neat little parlor. We were great friends, and had many a pleasant chat together. Sometimes the conversation would turn upon religious subjects. His tenets were those of the sceptic, and all his belief was confined to the natural. Of the future his highest conception was that he would not have to work mines, keep hotels or run a lodging house. In this respect he did not differ from the Indian, who looks upon hunting as the occupation of departed souls. He entertained, in a word, rather hazy views of the state of man after his death, but declared that death was as a sleep, that it had no terrors for him and that he would face it without emotion. In the event, however, it was pretty well shown that he feared the universal messenger, and that although life had burned down to the ashes, he hoped to live a little longer. He was appalled by the thought of leaving the world. I shall not forget the day I sat beside his cot in the old lodging house, endeavoring to inspire him with hope in the future. Despair was written on every line in his face, and his wild eye seemed to be searching for some ray of light. But of hope there was none for him; and the old man, worn out by a long illness, pleaded piteously for escape from the deathly reaper. There, with eyes fast set, short, quick breathing, sharp jerks of the limbs, he tossed upon his couch, clutching the bedclothes and writhing in the last agony. It was a fearful sight. It seemed like a literal interpretation of the words of the apostle, "It is a terrible thing to fall into the hands of the living God." With his closely-drawn features, and his glazed eye apparently fastened upon me, I was deeply moved at a situation which contained none of the consoling features of the deathbed of the Christian. But, of course, there is no limit to the uncovenanted mercies of God, Who knows the clay of which His creatures are made. Still I felt a certain sadness at the painful struggles of one who departed this life without the supernatural habits. I do not mean to

A DEVOTED MOTHER IN ADVERSITY

say that the unbeliever and sceptic always die in horror. Indeed, they sometimes pass away, as they came into the world, without any sign of consciousness, but the calmness and fortitude displayed by them are of a stoical cast, and devoid of the true spirit of resignation which is expressed by the disciple of a revealed religion. At the moment of his departure from this life, the luminous truth breaks upon the thoughtful man, that there are two beings evident to him, God and himself; and from the standpoint of a merely natural religion, he must regard that God as a judge, clothed with terrors. At such a time the unbeliever feels "the soul-piercing reality of Lucretius," speaking of religion and the threatening character it wears in the eyes of the infidel.

As the thirsty traveler welcomes the inviting spring, so do I hail the transition of my theme from the sombre side of life, fashioned after the purely natural, to the sunny side of life patterned upon the supernatural. In the second year of my missionary labors in the southwest, a Mrs. K—— came to the San Juan. She was a native of Manchester, England, and the mother of five children, left to her by a penniless husband, who, at the early age of thirty, died of consumption. For two years after his death she toiled hard at the great manufacturing centre. During the day she entrusted the little ones to the care of a feeble old grandma, who tottered around on her crutch, taking oatmeal and milk, with a little bread and tea, three times a day, rather than apply for more nutritious food at the workhouse. So, the little pale-faced woman, day by day trudged to and from the mill, making barely enough to save the children from starvation during the week and give them a decent dinner on Sunday. Retiring late to bed and rising early, she snatched a few minutes from the long hours of her daily task to mend the thin garments of her fatherless children and instil into their minds the principles of religion. As some satisfaction for her motherly attention she beheld her children always neat and clean, and far above the average children in those poverty-stricken districts. Being a woman of good conscience and some culture, she realized her obligations to give her girls a practical training, suitable to equip them for the duties of life. The eldest girl at the age of twelve began to assist her mother in providing for the family. The mother and daughter managed their domestic affairs so well that they were enabled to put aside a few dollars. A year later Mrs. K—— sent the two eldest girls to night school, that they might acquire a knowledge of the arts of housekeeping and fine sewing. They made rapid progress, and at the end of two years, the older one graduating with distinction, was appointed assistant teacher at the school.

Mrs. K—— had a brother in the San Juan who was always writing to her of the grand opportunities of this country. His letters were replete with the accounts of success and wealth in a land where the poor became rich, the weak strong and all sorts of diseases cured,

"Where a man is a man, if he is willing to toil,
And the humblest may gather the fruits of the soil."

Mrs. K——'s life was wearing out slowly but surely in the close atmosphere of the mills. The dread finger of consumption had begun to trace its first lines in her wan face. Why should she

A DEVOTED MOTHER IN ADVERSITY

not go to America, where she would have at least fresh air? Encouraged by the letters of her brother, who sent her the requisite passage money, she packed up her few belongings, and, with her children, set out for the bright land of the San Juan, which she reached in midwinter. The entire mountain region lay under many feet of snow, and for days and weeks the trains between Silverton and Durango were blocked. It took a large body of men three weeks to clear the track from the effects of a snowslide which had come down into the Animas canon. What a contrast to the mild winter of England! After many untoward events Mrs. K—— arrived at Silverton, where she engaged a modest residence for herself and her family. Beginnings are described as small, and they were very small in the case of an invalid who had very limited resources. The weather was extremely cold, fuel high, and provisions dear; so, the few dollars she brought with her from England were soon spent. Looking around for some aid in her distress, she received a lesson which comes to most people sooner than they expect, that friendship does not wear best in adversity. Mrs. K——, however, had studied in a good school, and learned to bear the trials of life with becoming composure. One of the sources of her affliction was the want of weekly mass and Sunday-school for her daughters. While she labored assiduously to supply these deficiencies by teaching her children herself, her heart was ready to break at the thought that she had left home and kind friends for a land of strangers. No one can fail to observe that the great masses of humanity are ever ready for change, purely and simply, without regard to even temporal gain. Men leave comfortable homes to find the sources of the Nile, or track the alligator in the swamps, for adventure. And it is a wise dispensation of Providence, stagnation being the death of progress. How often is utter indifference to results, the practical answer to the admonition of prudence, which embodies experience in the familiar saying: "You may go farther, and fare worse!"

The long dreary winter made way for the soft warm sunshine of spring. But Mrs. K—— continued to sink. The hollow cough and the hectic flush told of the ravages of the fatal disease, and lead so many to the delusive belief that death has not planted its standard on their perishing system. Rallying slightly with the change of season, she resolved to go to Rico, at the time a lively camp, where there was a pretty fair prospect of earning a livelihood. Upon her arrival at that town, she found that houses were at a premium, so it was hard to secure a dwelling at any price. After much hunting around, she succeeded in renting a small cabin on the Dolores, a few miles from Rico. Here she lived all summer. The girls, who were experts with the needle, made heavy flannel shirts and socks, which they readily sold to the miners. Thus passed the summer, and with good management, sufficient money was saved to tide the family over the winter. Mrs. K—— was made happy by seeing in her children the fruits of her judicious methods of education. Instead of foolishly striving to load them down with frivolous accomplishments, of which they were never likely to make profitable use, she trained their hands and eyes to remunerative employment. She felt

A DEVOTED MOTHER IN ADVERSITY

bound in conscience to procure for them such a training as would enable them to support themselves. Her knowledge of life taught her that what business success demands is not the ability to shine in declamation, play the pretty in the parlor, or loll upon a divan, dreaming of the fool's paradise, in which the chief diversion is "sipping the wine of Ispahan;" but that manual industrial schooling is what the majority of boys and girls need to enjoy a fair measure of happiness here and, it may be said, a better prospect of happiness hereafter. There are, even in our day of general advancement, some departures from the true scheme of enlightenment. "By its fruits ye shall know the tree," and it is not wide of the mark to say, that the state would not be so deeply infected with socialism and the other prevailing isms, if the practical received a more careful consideration in the plans of education. Many young men, after spending long years poring over books at academy or college, are disappointed on the threshold of life, at not being appreciated at college standards, and obliged to seek positions, in competition with the less favored crowd, who have little book learning, but some common sense. A few years, however, teach the distinguished graduate that while poetry and eloquence adorn the high places, won by persevering toil, employers generally seek not brilliant scholars, but industrious, reliable workers. The sooner our youth learn that they must begin at the bottom of the ladder and under the wholesome discipline of hard knocks work to the top, the sooner they will fit themselves for prosperous careers. Young women, too, learn that "life is real, life is earnest," and wholly unlike the beguiling descriptions of "mansions in the moon," which fill the pages of an ephemeral literature. The last panic that befell this country revealed many of the hidden workings of a false system of economics, and emphasizes the fact that we are in a new era of development. The people of the United States are ancestors themselves, and in a constant state of evolution, framing by successful experiment, a destiny, unthought of by past generations. We have broken away from the cast-iron theories and straight lines of our forefathers. This is an accomplished fact, and our methods are different from those of Europe. We begin where the people of Europe have left off. We recognize woman as the equal not the inferior of man, and many of the states have removed the common law disabilities of the woman. A wit has remarked that woman was superior to man, now she is only his equal. Without considering the merits of this change from the traditions of the past, or pretending to discuss the wisdom of this policy, it is sufficient to say that in most of our cities, women are found in offices and positions which, twenty years ago, were filled by men only. As women then have enlarged opportunities of usefulness, they must equip themselves for their new duties. But they must not forget that they are women, as well as citizens, and that their first duty is to preside over the home as its queen, not usurping, but sharing the authority of the natural head of the family. Besides the breadwinner there is a breadmaker, besides the clothweaver there is a clothpatcher, in short there must be a trained housekeeper, who keeps the dyspepsia from her husband and makes the most out of the least. In

A DEVOTED MOTHER IN ADVERSITY

the manual school, our girls should be taught to make a good loaf of bread, sew neatly, keep a house clean, help the young husband to establish himself in business, and perhaps to appreciate the wisdom of minding their own domestic affairs. But, of course, manual training is not a panacea for all the ills of life. The education of the hand and the eye is not sufficient. The heart must be educated, and education must be founded on principles of morality and religion. Without God there can be no commonwealth. Aristotle, in considering the comparative merits of different systems of government, maintains that without intelligence and virtue a republic cannot endure. I fully appreciate the prizes held out to those who obtain eminence in the higher arts and sciences, and that these prizes are worth striving for. In fine, it is the duty of the educator to impress upon the minds of the rising generation that any calling in life, whether high or low, is praiseworthy.

> "Honor and shame from no condition rise.
> Act well your part, there all the honor lies."

In the fall Mrs. K—— began to show symptoms of heart failure, and the physician ordered her at once to a lower altitude. On my arrival at Rico, her daughters informed me of her condition and requested me to go down to the little cabin, say mass, and prepare their dear mother for her last journey. I found the patient woman, frail and wasted, but calm and resigned. This world had lost its charms for her, and the world to come had no terrors for her. When she spoke of leaving her children, she said: "Why should I fret, since I receive all my afflictions from the hand of God. He is my father and their father, and in His care, my children are safe." The little parlor was clean and neat, with home-woven carpets upon the floor; and bunches of wild flowers, gathered from the mountains by the girls, gave the altar a bright appearance. Five candles of virgin white, decorated with delicate colors and encircled by crowns of artificial flowers, had been placed upon the altar. I remarked that two candles were enough, and inquired why these wreaths of roses were placed around the candles. "Oh Father," said the girls, "these are our first communion candles and crowns. We are making a small offering to our blessed Lord, just as we did at our first communion in Manchester. It is all we have to give Him. Mamma said we should make a complete offering of all we had, and here are our candles and flowers, and our better possessions, our souls and bodies."

The next morning, I said mass at five o'clock, and another candle and wreath were added to the group of lights, as the youngest child was about to receive her first holy communion. The story of the mother of the Maccabees came to my mind, as that Christian mother knelt with her children at the altar. There they were, six devout mortals, with tears streaming down their cheeks. I pronounced the solemn words: "Behold the Lamb of God, who takes away the sins of the world," and the confession of faith and humility: "Lord, I am not worthy that Thou shouldst enter under my roof, say but the word and my soul shall be healed," and gave them the Bread of Life. It was a sublime spectacle, which it is the privilege of the Christian religion alone to offer. I am frank

A DEVOTED MOTHER IN ADVERSITY

to confess that I was touched by the solemnity of the scene, as the dawn with silent step stole down from the gray peaks into the valley of the Dolores.

After breakfast, a ranchman drove up to the door of the cabin. We all assisted in packing the few effects of the family into the wagon, and in a short time, the little cabin on the Dolores was tenantless. Mrs. K—— was made as comfortable as possible, and accompanied by her daughters, set out to Cortez, where, in the Montezuma valley with its inferior altitude and milder winter, she fancied she might grow strong. I promised to visit her before the weather became too cold, and confer upon her again the consolations of our holy religion. "But man proposes and God disposes." She went east, where she died as became a woman who in affliction attained sanctity.

Saddling old Bill, I was soon on my way up the gulch, and winding along the narrow wagon road, which makes its way serpent-like on the side of the mountains to the Hermosa. The day was beautiful. The sunlight in flitting shadows was creeping higher and higher up the mountain. About noon I reached the Hermosa, unsaddled my horse aud picketed him in the long grass. While I was reclining in the shade and eating my lunch, a man came down the gulch riding a roan pony and urging on four tired looking burros laden with several sacks of ore, blankets, shovels, pans, picks, drills and the sheet iron stove which the miner always carries with him. A short-tailed dog, limping on three legs, brought up the rear of the sorry-looking caravan. The stranger halted at the stream, and dismounting, permitted the pony to plunge in and drink of the refreshing water. To meet a person in the wilds is a great blessing, and I saluted the man by remarking: "A pretty warm day." He recognized my salute and said: "Yes, awful hot for this time of the year," and lying down on his face, drank long and deep from the stream. Having fastened his pony, he walked over to me, and threw himself on the grass beside me. He was fully six feet three, and very muscular. He had long, red, unkempt hair and beard. With a hearty good will, he accepted my invitation to lunch. "You have been out prospecting" I said. "Yes, eight weeks now," he remarked, "and I've had a fearful time up there at the foot of those high mountains. I found some very good signs at the head of a little creek, and camped there. I washed out quite a bit of gold too," and he drew out of his pocket a large tobacco sack full of black sand and gold specks. "Yes, it was hard to get. There was no water of any account, and you cannot get the stuff without plenty of water. But I tell you I had lots of water the night before last; and but for the little mouse-colored burro over there I might have been killed or drowned. You see the gulch was very narrow, with steep banks on either side. We had a cloudburst. Such rain, great Cæsar! it came down in torrents, it fairly spilled over; it was more like a deluge than an ordinary rainstorm. I was curled up in my tent with Jerry, my dog, and trying to keep dry, when, all of a sudden, that old burro ran up to the tent and began to bray. The braying of the donkey, the peals of thunder and the barking of Jerry, made a terrible din. I got up and peering out, saw by the lightning that the

A DEVOTED MOTHER IN ADVERSITY

creek was rapidly filling up. The water was then close to the tent. I had no time to lose, so I rose quickly, pulled the pickets of the burros and barely got them to a place of safety when a mass of logs upset the tent and broke poor Jerry's leg. Yesterday I dug out my things and they look pretty tough, but I tell you were it not for that old burro I might have been a goner.'' I should feel I was doing an injustice to one of the inhabitants of the Rockies, were I to take only a passing notice of that humble, domestic animal, the burro, known in musical circles under the facetious appellation of the Rocky Mountain canary. I am free to state that I cannot give unstinted praise to his assaults upon the higher notes of the first tenor; for the quality of his voice would not recommend him to the manager of an operatic company, were he in quest of a good chorus. However, as a slight recognition of his valuable services to man in doubt and trial, I offer the following tribute:

THE BURRO

When Adam named in days of old,
The bird and beast and every fold,
He gave to each its proper class,
And well defined the gentle ass,
His ears made long, inclined to flap,
Down his shoulders is nature's strap.
Thus marked, he went o'er the world wide,
To help us all by easy stride.
Docile, humble, of low degree,
Destined ever a slave to be,
He took his place when time began,
And since has been the friend of man.
From Eastern climes he made his way,
Where his'try marks his longest stay,
And to the West, o'er ocean's main,
With Adam's sons he swelled the train;

IN THE SAN JUAN

But man, like ever-shifting fame,
Resolved to change the donkey's name.
Away on mountain, far from throng,
The sound he made, man called a song.
So, moved by notes, most deem scary,
Some dub him now the new canary.

From early morn to close of day,
He sings his song the same old way.
His voice is harsh, a choking roar,
And fills the mind with thoughts of gore.
His notes,—one short, with two quite long,
Contain the burden of his song.
At midnight hour when nature rests,
His crooning bray breaks out the best,
And o'er the crags and passes bleak,
His voice resounds in dismal shriek,
And some will cry when they are airy,
That "He's a bird—a true canary."
The burro is his Spanish name,
And bearing it he rose to fame;
For up and down 'neath driver's wrath,
He climbs with load on narrow path,
Where slipp'ry trails and icy slate
Precipitate him to his fate.
Plodding along at break of day,
So, year by year he makes his way,
Loaded heavy in mountain dust,
In winter's snows, and clouds that burst.
Keeping his pace in sun and rain,
He creeps along, a mountain train.
In hunger, they say, oft he can,
When all is gone, consume a can.
Bridles, saddles and boxes too;
He'll also eat a soleless shoe.
Flour and coffee, bacon and ham,
He looks upon, as we do jam.
Butter and cheese left in the shade,
Will disappear on his parade.
Trousers and shirts, in time of need,
Make him a meal for sharpest greed.
But of the things beyond his skill
Are iron hammer, miner's drill.
Around the camp he always goes
Striking at dogs and kindred foes,

A DEVOTED MOTHER IN ADVERSITY

Braying aloud with great delight
When hay abounds and grain's in sight;
Sometimes limping from saddle sore
Dug in his back by sacks of ore.
Taking ills like a patient man,
He spends his time the best he can,
Careless of wounds and battered feet,
Stumbling along the stony street;
Or, standing meek, with load or pack,
Eats the hay from his partner's back.

When flowers bloom and days are fine,
The burro keeps in better line.
When roads are good, and grass is long,
With stomach full he pegs along;
And o'er the hills and craggy walls
He carries nymphs from Vassar's halls.
'Neath Harvard's sports, or men from Yale,
The same old wag is in his tail.
The schoolmarms, too, both young and old,
Ride him up through the mountains bold.
His faithfulness should prompt us so
To treat him well where e'er we go.
A friend to all on dreary pass,
Most useful is the modest ass.

EIGHTH SKETCH

SOME of San Juan's winters are very severe, while others are comparatively mild, but on account of the dryness of the atmosphere the cold is not felt so much as it is on the plains. Month after month, from late in the spring to the latter part of August, the snow melts slowly and the mountain torrents pour down the gulches and over the plains, irrigating the farms and insuring bountiful crops. Hence, the farmer watches the winter's storm with joy, while the miner, fearing the snowslide and the precipice, dreads its approach. The winter of 1890, setting in betimes, was long and bitter. The rocks and mountain sides were covered with deep snow, and the tall pines, with their fleecy coat of white, looked small. The roads were blocked and often almost impassable. Moses Livermann, the director of the Silverton Railroad, was pushed to the utmost to keep the line open until Christmas. A large number of men had been at work from October, and a bank on either side of the road was so piled up with snow that no more could be thrown over. The Silverton Railroad, one of the highest in the world, connects Ironton with Silverton. I went over to Silverton from Ouray in October. It was, I think, on the 3d, and I rode part of the way to Ironton on a sleigh. I was not a party of one, but one of a party of travelers, and it took us from 10:30 a. m. to 6:30 p. m. to reach Red Mountain, a distance of about four miles. We had only two cars, one of which was derailed at least six times that day, and all hands assisted in removing the snow and in prying on the car.

THE BLASPHEMER'S FATE

When we were about ready to continue our journey to Silverton I was stopped by a telephone message calling me back to Ouray, which message stated that a man was dying at the hospital. I was compelled to procure a horse at the livery stable and return as fast as I could. It was a trying task, but I arrived at Ouray without a mishap. Some time after, upon trying to visit Silverton under similar difficulties, I came near losing my life. The Ouray toll road was banked up with masses of snow. While passing over one of the bad spots in the road the sleigh tipped over, spilling out the passengers. I happened to be on the precipice side, and was thrown down the abrupt declivity some forty feet. Here the snow proved a friend to me, for it saved me from bruises, and perhaps death. My fellow-passengers pulled me up with a long rope, and we kept on our way just as if nothing unusual had taken place.

Around Silverton, especially near Howardsville, snowslides often play havoc. In a wild wreck of rocks, railroad ties, time-worn boulders and broken trees, a slide, on one occasion, nearly carried away the depot at Silverton. It is, therefore, one of the first considerations of the miner to mark well the lay of the mountains, before he builds his cabin.

In the summer of 1890 three young fellows came from the east, staked a claim, and began to run a tunnel into one of the mountains of this locality. It was not long before they learned to appreciate the perils of the snowslide. At least one of the miners was a Catholic; but, as will be seen, a reproach to his religion. He had been a student in a college, had served on the altar, and been tenderly bred by Christian parents; but, setting small store by the advantages he possessed at home, he went to the far-off land, where, removed from wholesome restraint, he forsook the observances of his religion. No words were too obscene, no oath was too horrible, and no blasphemy too indecent for a youth upon whose early days the light of fair promise shone. It was his greatest pleasure to take the Holy Name in vain, and companions of his, who had no religious training, shuddered, when compelled to listen to his foul language. It had been storming for several days, and many feet of snow rested upon the mountain side. It needs but a faint breeze then to send the whole mass down the mountain, and woe betide whatever is in its track. The three young men had been working in the tunnel all day, and were about to return to their cabin, which was about 200 yards across a gulch. The freshly fallen snow far up the mountain side was glistening in the last rays of the winter's sun. All around was pure and white, and not a sound broke the stillness, save the voices of the three young miners, who, as they scanned the mountain and weighed the chances of an avalanche, were discussing the expediency of crossing the gulch. Our nominal Catholic, having gazed on the scene for awhile, decided to face the danger. His friends remonstrated with him, but for their objections he had only reproaches and curses, and calling them cowards for their prudence, he swore that he would cross that gulch in spite of Christ Himself. So, leaving his companions still undecided in the mouth of the tunnel, he set forth by himself. He had passed about half way over when one of

THE REMAINS OF A SNOW-SLIDE

THE BLASPHEMER'S FATE

his friends moved after him, the third one, however, standing in the tunnel and awaiting results. Scarcely had the second member of the party advanced fifty yards, when the mighty mass broke loose from the mountain with a thunderous roar that would awaken the dead, and rolled down and on like the churning waves of Lake Michigan when swept by the fiercest storm. Despair seized the young men; there was no hope for them. How in five feet of snow could they flee from that avalanche, which grew in speed and volume as it rushed down the mountain side? In a trice it was upon them, and dashed over their lifeless bodies in less time than it takes to record their fate. It is said that a rock struck the unhallowed blasphemer, and ground into mince meat that tongue of his which had so often defied the God who made him. It was an appropriate punishment, and a warning against sins of the tongue. "Blessed tongue that spoke the praises of God," cried St. Bonaventure, as he kissed that sacred relic of the good St. Anthony of Padua, but accursed is the tongue that becomes the organ of blasphemy. This reminds me of a similar incident in this same country. Two miners were working in a tunnel, and having drilled a hole, loaded it. From some cause the fuse failed to ignite the cap and the shot did not go off. One of the miners, a man of ungovernable temper, vented his spleen on the broken fuse in a torrent of oaths, and wound up his abuse by cursing the Almighty. He grasped the hammer and drill and began in a frantic manner to unload the hole. His partner fled, lest the charge might explode before he had time to get away. It did explode and tore the mad miner to pieces, eviscerating him and strewing his intestines on the ground before his face. It was a horrible sight. His partner tried to make the dying miner as comfortable as possible. When he came to his senses, which was not for some time, the unfortunate man acknowledged his guilt. His earnest petition was that God might forgive him for this sin of blasphemy, which was so speedily punished. Thus two blasphemers died, like the thieves on the cross, one to all appearances repentant, the other, God knows how, but "His words will be justified and His judgments will prevail."

Ouray was dull that winter, for the boys seldom descended the mountains. Sneffles was hidden in storm-laden clouds, and the highest peak in the district, on whose tapering heights snow is seen the year round, looked flat and dumpish in the heaps of snow that remained upon it. To come down from the Virginius mine was to invite great danger, and even at Christmas few dared seek the season's festivities or the refreshment of Mother Buchanan's bath house. Here is a boiling spring, which is one of the sights of the town, and many an afflicted miner has had the rheumatism dislodged from his bones in the big swimming pool of hot water which bubbles fresh from the earth at Mother Buchanan's. The water is hot enough to boil eggs, so it always needs tempering with the cold water which is provided in the bathing rooms. Every one calls Mrs. Buchanan mother and Mr. Buchanan the general, and a finer old couple do not live. Mother came from sweet Donegal, and brought with her a heart brim full of sympathy and good humor, and well she deserved her title of endear-

THE BLASPHEMER'S FATE

ment, for she was a mother to all, and few knew her better than the writer. As for the general, frank and openhearted that he was, there was nothing in the house too good for his friends, who were all who had the happiness of knowing him. He was so civil and obliging that if he had no spring water at hand—and he loved spring water—he would take a bucket and make a bee line for the adjoining hostlery of Pat Hess, who had it on tap. So frequent were the general's accommodating trips to his neighbors that in the summer, when the boys in great force invaded the bath house, fifty to sixty taking baths on Saturday afternoons, a well-beaten path led to the business place of Mr. Hess. This gentleman was a German, but how he got the name Pat, unless he was born in Ireland on his way from Germany, I cannot say. The general was one of the old timers in Ouray, having come to the camp before there was a wagon road to the town. Camp life was the general's delight. With a good rifle, some flour, bacon, coffee and sugar, frying pan and spring water he was master of the situation.

That winter a mine contractor, who hauled most of the ore from the Virginius and returned with supplies, lost a great many mules. They perished in the snowslides, or, tumbling over the precipice, were killed. The Virginius, which was at an elevation of about 13,000 feet above sea level, was approached by a narrow, difficult trail. My tried and true friend, Billy Maher, had a mining property, yes I believe half a dozen properties, near by, called for everything that was patriotic, from "The Wearing of the Green" to "Brian Boru." Billy was a hustler. He

IN THE SAN JUAN

had been in the mountains six or seven years before I met him and had prospected all over the Sneffles district, where he staked his claims and worked assessments for Uncle Sam. Close to the apex of the Rockies he erected his cabin. There were no trees or grass, as it was far above timber line. It was a desolate place, rocks, rocks, rocks, on all sides. The only signs of life were a peculiar species of ground hog, that seemed to thrive on fresh air and the shrill whistling, which might be taken for a kind of don't-tread-on-the-tail-of-my-coat bravado, and an interesting little creature known to mountaineers under the name of the stone marten, whose continuous barking serves as a kind of second fiddle in concert. Of a brown color, with a pug-shaped head, close-fitting ears, and a pocket-gopher tail, this nervous little animal, which always gives warning of its approach, flits with the agility of a chipmunk from rock to rock in search of grass and roots.

The sportsman would deem it strange to find wild duck on the tops of the Rocky Mountains. Yet it is a fact that the hardy little teal dwells on the lakes that nestle like jeweled caskets above timber line. Here they lay their eggs, hatch their young, and feed on the countless fish which swarm in those remote reservoirs. How the fish ever got there, is one of the mysteries hidden from the modern historian. However, it may be presumed that the aborigines made those lakes their summer resorts and stocked them with fish from the valley streams, or the mountain torrent, which only the trout can ascend. Twenty years ago, in many of Colorado's streams, it was no sport to fish and hunt. Shoals of the finny tribe moved about in their native element, shutting out the

THE BLASPHEMER'S FATE

light from the transparent waters, and devouring one another in pursuit of food. To catch three and four at a time, was an ordinary thing. They are not so numerous now, but good fishing may still be had, and offers rare sport to a person who loves to play and catch the gamiest of all fishes. With the first approaches of spring, and after the snow has melted slowly, the teal may be seen making its way from the lower altitudes up the stream. In the early summer it builds its nest on the sedgy bank of some little lake and there rears its young. Should these swift and experienced explorers be mistaken in their prognostications of the weather and happen to be caught in the blinding snow, they often lose their bearings and fall ready victims to the inclemency of the weather. Flying around in the thick snow they alight in the pines or fall exhausted in the drifts, where they are soon covered up, perish of hunger or freeze to death. Farther down the mountain, among the stunted red willows which separate the naked rocks from the first signs of vegetation, is the home of the ptarmigan, commonly known as the Rocky Mountain quail. It is a beautiful bird, and twice the size of the much-praised bob-white. In winter it becomes as white as snow, and at times can scarcely be discerned in the snow. In summer its color changes from a white to a brown, streaks of white remaining on the neck and wings. The feet are covered down to the toes with a thick, heavy coat of feathers, which afford ample protection from the most severe weather. The ptarmigan, as it moves only a short distance at a time, falls an easy prey to the hunter.

In the same region dwells the mountain grouse,

which is somewhat larger than the prairie chicken and not unlike it in appearance, having a long tail and a rather dignified strut. When disturbed, it will fly up into a tree and wait to be shot. In avoiding the hunter it never manifests the cunning of the prairie chicken. Whole coveys of these birds have been shot in the trees, not a single one seeking to make its escape. In the winter it lives like the ptarmigan, on the buds of the willows, or moves down into the valleys where food is plentiful. In the same locality is found the snow-shoe rabbit. This animal is about the size of the ordinary jack rabbit, but of a more delicate constitution. It dwells far up in the pines at the edge of timber line. It is probable that it received its name, snow shoe, from the webbed formation of its feet. Its toes are very short and the foot is broad and covered with long matted hair, which, growing between the toes, gives the feet a bulky form that enables this denizen of the Rockies swiftly to run over the freshly fallen snow without sinking.

Billy's cabin was about ten by fifteen feet, and was constructed of native lumber. A small cellar had been quarried out of the rock for potatoes and other vegetables, but Billy generally brought the potatoes to bed with him, otherwise they might freeze in the cellar. For water he used snow in the winter, and in summer, springs on the mountain are almost as plentiful as wild flowers. Every miner can make biscuits, flapjacks and a sort of white hoe cake. The miner is a good liver; he buys a whole steer, or beef by the quarter, hangs it up high, where, frozen solid, it will remain safe and fresh for eight months of the year. Besides, putrefaction at a great altitude is

THE BLASPHEMER'S FATE

very slow, so there is no lack of fresh meat in the miner's bill of fare, though bacon or ham is most used, as it seasons a meal. Billy married a little body from his native country and settled down in life. Everyone wished him joy, and all Ouray turned out to do honor to his wedding day. His marriage did not impair, but rather increased his activity in working his properties, and he expected to strike it rich soon. Fall lengthened into the harsh winter of which I have been writing, and Billy was unable to come down as often as before to Ouray. At Christmas, however, he risked the dangers of the descent; surely it would not be like Christmas without Billy and his honest greeting: "How are you, anyhow?" About the middle of February he paid the town his last visit and remarked that he had had an awful time getting down from the Virginius mine. As usual, he assisted at mass and received the Blessed Eucharist with all the devotion of his pious soul.

Upon his return to the mine he took with him a beautiful English pointer of mine called Prince. He loved the dog and the dog loved him. While Billy and his partner, who hailed from sunny Italy, worked all day in the tunnel, Prince guarded the cabin. Everything was moving smoothly with the partners, and the prospects of a splendid strike were good, when a shocking calamity befell Billy.

> "Ne'er unmixed with grief has heaven
> Its joys on mortals shed."

It is an unfortunate custom of miners to take giant powder into their cabins, hold it by the fire and thaw it out. When frozen it will not explode, but when thawed it is one of the most dangerous and powerful explosives. On the 25th of February, Billy, before setting out for the mine, was engaged thawing the powder, when all of a sudden eight sticks of the powder went off. The result was appalling, the stove was blown through the roof and the cabin was demolished, but the partners, where were they? Billy was horribly mangled, his right hand was torn out of shape. It was in this hand he held a stick of giant powder at the time of the accident, yet not a bone was broken, but the fingers were laid bare, the flesh having been blown off, and both eyes were destroyed. His face appeared as if painted with powder; all his clothing was torn into shreds and the discharge hurled him under the bunk. His partner, who was washing the dishes at the time, was not much hurt, but he received a painful shock and some slight injuries. After a considerable time the Italian came to himself and shouted with all his strength for Billy. There was no answer, and he thought his partner must be dead. At last he lifted his eyelid with his finger, thus keeping his eye open, and saw Billy lying in a heap under the bunk. Slowly rising he dragged himself over to where Billy lay, and shaking the recumbent figure, roused his wounded friend, who faintly whispered, "Wrap me in a blanket and bring help."

It was only a mile to the Terrible mine, but there were so many feet of snow on the ground that it was impossible to accomplish the short distance without snow shoes. The Italian knew nothing about snow shoes, and, therefore, was unable to use them on his feet. Picking them up he put his hands into the straps designed for the feet and set out to swim over the sea of snow,

THE BLASPHEMER'S FATE

which in swelling waves followed the rise and fall of the land. The trail was down hill most of the way, with here and there obstructions in the shape of rocks smothered with snow. When he encountered these he was compelled to swim around them. Using the shoes to keep him afloat, and his feet as propellers, he shortened the distance to the Terrible.

Meanwhile Prince was alone with his master in the cabin, of which only the floor and one end remained. When the dog saw the Italian go away, he returned to the wrecked cabin, moaned piteously for some time, smelled of his blood-stained friend, and then sent up a howl that was most pathetic. He then climbed upon the side of the house that lay far out on the snow drift, and directed his gaze to the Humbolt mine. This mine was not so far away as the Terrible, but was much higher up, and that is why Billy's partner did not try to reach it. Prince sniffed the air for a moment, then gave a short bark and plunged into the deep snow toward the Humbolt, between which and the Terrible was a trail fairly well opened by the packers and miners, going to and returning from Ouray. A hill hid Billy's cabin from this trail, so no one could learn of the disaster, and the thunder sound of dynamite is so common in the mountains that no special notice would be taken of it. Prince pressed on through the snow, resting now and then, and turning back longing eyes to the wrecked abode of his master. At last he came within sight of the trail. A miner was making his way over the drifted road when his attention was called to the barking of the beautiful dog. Indeed, he was beautiful, being of the regulation kind, black and white, with long ears and large eyes which beamed with intelligence. The moment a gun was taken down he was at hand, licked the gun and fawned on the sportsman for permission to go hunting, and sometimes he would lie in wait for a hunting party until he had a chance to join in the sport. When he saw the man on the trail he set up a cry of distress, and sitting in the snow, moaned, then suddenly turned back a short distance. He wanted to engage the miner's attention and kept running up closer, continuing to bark, then retreated, but the miner did not understand his strange movements and kept the uneven tenor of his way. As a last resort, Prince came straight in front of him, barking savagely and snarling in his mad endeavor to turn the man to Billy's cabin. The miner was somewhat afraid of what he thought was a vicious dog, and made several kicks at him. Finally Prince retreated, made his way back to the cabin and lay crouching beside the couch of his master, who could not see or hear him, the detonation of the powder having deafened him; and both eyes were destroyed.

The Italian, in the meantime, swam down hill on the Norwegian shoes until he came to the bottom of the gulch, when he had to climb up the mountain several hundred yards. On his way he could almost look into the boarding house of the Terrible mine, but no one saw him. Half the men were working, the other half sleeping, and the cooks were busy preparing dinner. The poor fellow, wet to the neck and ready to give up from exhaustion, still plunged on, using the long snow shoes as staves to drag his half paralyzed body up the steep incline. It was three in the afternoon when he arrived at the Terrible, having started from the cabin at about 7:30.

When he informed the miners of the accident a party of four was speedily organized to convey the mangled miner to Ouray. The little band proceeded at once to the Virginius, took the trail which leads to the Humbolt, and then the route Prince had taken. All had snow shoes and the trip was made without serious trouble. Arrived at the dismantled cabin, they found Billy and the dog side by side in the splintered bunk. They hastily constructed a hand sled, and strapping Billy, Esquimau-like, on the sled, covered him up. Two of the party took the lead and two more kept behind, holding a rope fastened to the sled to keep it from tipping over. In this manner they started back to the Terrible. It was now growing dark and the wind began to blow a gale. Sometimes the location of the mine was lost, and as the advancing darkness and the howling storm gathered around them, they trembled with fear. One of the men broke his snow shoe, another was so worn out that he wished to be left behind until help arrived, but the other two, inured to mountain travel, forced their companions to go on. Just before entering the gulch they heard the crash of a snowslide away to the right. It can easily be told from the explosion of dynamite, as it comes with a dull, heavy thud, devoid of all resonance. At last, ready to drop, they arrived at the Terrible. Four men had been notified at the Virginius to be at hand to relieve the first squad of helpers and take Billy down to Porter's. The Virginius was only a short distance from the Terrible. Four volunteers cheerfully responded to the call and prepared for the journey to

Porter's, which was three miles down the mountain. But they never reached the Terrible; they were lost in a snowslide. As the four men failed to reach the Terrible, the same miners, fatigued though they were, resumed the task of bearing Billy to the hospital at Ouray. It was quite a heroic effort for the four men without relief to accomplish the whole journey from Billy's cabin to Ouray. When they came back the next afternoon they met one of the men from the Virginius and reproached him for not having sent the promised help, thus compelling them to carry the wounded man the whole way. "We did send four men," he said, "at dusk yesterday evening." They all instinctively turned and looked down the mountain side. There they beheld the track of an awful snowslide and knew the fate of the four miners. Looking closely they saw a hat on the snow, and following the track of the slide soon came to a hand, frozen stiff, protruding from the snow. They digged around it carefully and presently reached the head of a man. The man was standing up as straight as an arrow with his hands thrown out, as if to ward off a crushing blow, or perhaps to keep them free from that horrible snow packing which ensues, when the crunching mass closes around an object. I remember the case of the victim of a snowslide who had worked his way through the mass of snow with his fingers, and when he issued from the living tomb was fingerless, the fingers having been worn out in the effort to free himself. The first man who was uncovered was a Mr. M——, a powerful fellow. He may have lived five or six hours standing up in his snowy tomb, and no doubt shouting for help, for there was a

THE BLASPHEMER'S FATE

large cavity which had been thawed out by his warm breath. By degrees he was frozen to death, but the struggle for life must have been supreme. Held as if by a vise, he must have fought a fierce battle for life. The only hope for a person caught in a snowslide is to remain on the top of the snow, which advances like the waves of the ocean in its ebb and flow. If you are thrown down at the outset your chances of life are next to nothing. Mr. M—— seems to have ridden the snow for some time, but the grinding mass submerged him. The next body found was that of a poor miner from Delta, Colorado, who had gone to the big mine to make a few dollars to buy seed for his ranch and help support a wife and six children. His neck was broken, so he scarcely knew what happened. The other two members of the ill-fated party must have been killed outright.

Poor Billy Maher was brought to the sisters' hospital that night about eleven o'clock. The physician examined him and found that he was blind and internally injured. The explosion almost destroyed his hearing, and to make myself heard by him I had to speak at the top of my voice. I could gather from his faint whispers that he did not think he was very much injured, but he said that if he was blind he would rather die than live. We entertained hopes of his recovery for a day or two, but they were in vain. Billy was slowly dying, so I gave him the last sacraments of the church and prepared him for death. He repeated some of the prayers and continued to make ejaculations expressive of his love of God, until he could do so no longer. Gradually, he sank into a state of insensibility. As the gray dawn of morning stole over the eastern mountains Billy's heart went silent to the touch of death, the weary march of life was done, and on the powder-begrimed face a deathly pallor settled. Billy was no more, and the little cabin beyond the ocean in distant Tipperary would never again be visited by one, whose fondest hope was that he might sit once more beneath the thatched roof of his childhood's home.

At Billy's funeral nearly everyone in town was present. My heart was too full for utterance; I could make no formal address, and only said that his life was more eloquent than any sermon I could preach. It is the simple truth to say that the dead man's part in life was well played. "He had a tear for pity and a hand open as day for works of mercy." He loved to serve mass and to minister to the wants of the priest, and in his goings in and goings out he was so well approved that greater honor could not be shown to a public official. His best desire was satisfied when he died fortified by the rights of the church, which he loved better than his own life. The memory of this noble soul deserves this tribute, and will long be cherished by his friends. "Only the actions of the just smell sweet and blossom in the dust," and merit record to enlighten others.

A MINER'S DEATH

'Tis dreary to-night on the mountain,
  The starlight is hid in the sky,
The thick snow is falling and drifting,
  From each rugged peak's point on high.

Away on Mount Sneffles bare summits,
  Where nature so awesome appears,
Where the gloom-shaded face of the morn
  Distracts the beholder with fears,

THE BLASPHEMER'S FATE

A miner is dying and praying,
   That God in his mercy may send
The Soggarth Aroon to his cabin,
   A sinner in need to befriend.

Meanwhile in the black winter's storm,
   His partner makes haste the long day,
To announce a miner is dying
   On the mountain, from help far away.

No mother, no wife to watch o'er him,
   And calm the worn spirit's unrest,
Or lift up the soul that's aweary,
   By whisp'ring to him of the blest.

*   *   *   *   *   *

The unction has now touched the Christian,
   His lips are still moist from the oil,
Scarce has absolution been giv'n,
   When nature succumbs to the toil.

The crucifix clasped to his bosom,
   A tear on his cheek lately shed,
A word for his mother and family,
   The soul of the miner has fled.

Beside him we watched from the midnight,
   Till heaven unlocked the new day,
We laid him to rest on the hillside,
   From home and dear friends far away.

The long train of sleighs and carriages moved slowly down the street and then wound through the gulch to Portland until it came to the cemetery, where, with the final prayers of the church, we consigned the remains of Billy Maher to their last resting place—

> "The tender tear which Nature sheds
> O'er those we love we drop into his grave."

NINTH SKETCH

THE story of the prodigal son is repeated every day, and will continue to be repeated, until sin is no more. Every family has its black sheep. No one knows this better than the priest, whose ear is ever open to the story of man's folly. In his missionary calls, which summon him day and night to perform the task of reconciliation between God and man, the dying prodigal, returning to his father's house with tears in his eyes, is a familiar figure. The cloak of charity is sometimes thrown over worthless lives, so that friends may not be offended, or pious ears scandalized. When a disedifying life escapes due criticism, religion is mocked at, and becomes a by-word of reproach. Charity to the dead may be injustice to the living, and the young are likely to be deceived by the glamor of the public funeral. The pagan crystallized a gracious sentiment, when he observed, that nothing but what is good should be spoken of the dead; but the true principle is found in the wise injunction: "Let justice be done, though the heavens should fall." If men practised justice more generally in their dealings with their fellowmen, it would not be necessary to bolster up character by the display of a charity, which, unenlivened by supernatural motives, degenerates into sensuality.

While I was on the missions of the San Juan, I met many who belonged to the category of prodigals, who are usually spendthrifts, but sometimes misers, "in whom there is nothing heavenly." I wish to mention one or two instances of the spendthrift class. John W —— had fought from Bull Run to Antietam, and was wounded three times; but the final stroke was reserved for him at Ouray, when encamped on the field with the enemy that gives no quarter. He owned by gift or sale some mining property in the Ouray Gold Belt, and had come west to see it. He had a considerable sum of money, as he drew a pretty liberal pension from the inexhaustible coffers of generous Uncle Sam. He bore on his body as mementoes of the war and a consideration for his pension, three bullet wounds, one of which was very painful, breaking out with assured regularity. This wound he received on the gory field of Antietam, where, for two days, he lay with his head on the breast of a dead comrade. He came to Ouray at a moment when there was much excitement over the American-Nettie discovery. It was a time when every day saw newcomers, by tens and twenties, drop into town to locate and buy claims. So eager in the pursuit of new finds were these mine seekers, that not a few of them lay at night in the snow to secure first choice in the diggings. The people of Ouray congratulated themselves upon the fact that their city was not subject to booms, but kept a steady, healthy growth.

More or less gold had been discovered in the mountains adjacent to the city, and a little even in the streets of the town. When the boys came down from the mines for rest and recuperation, they often took hammers and drills, and strolled up into the Blow Out or Gold Belt. They located some very good prospects, which showed a fair quantity of the yellow metal. It remained, however, for a couple of good-natured fellows to make one of the best strikes in the Blow Out. When money was plentiful they spent it freely, and, when short of funds, borrowed from their friends. They referred with pride to their future prospects, especially in the Gold Belt, which they claimed, would some day create a great sensation. So they pounded away at the tunnel in the Blow Out, avoiding the dangers of the higher altitudes and enjoying the privilege of being their own masters.

One day they came down to Ouray with a sack of the volcanic stuff, which fairly set the town wild. It assayed far up into the thousands, and everyone in town rushed up to the Belt to stake a claim. The news spread to the east, and mining experts poured into the town to examine the new find. Large sums were offered for a location, and soon the eastern side of the canon was dotted with tents. Our lucky young men sold out for over $40,000 in cash, and were looked upon as the heroes of the hour. One of them having some strange ideas of his own, the first resolution he took was to go down into New Mexico and undertake to break all the faro banks. Full of this strange resolution he set out and remained away three months, returning with the loss of several thousand dollars. Not learning anything from his failure in New Mexico, he continued in his stubborn resolve to "wind up," as he said, the faro banks of Ouray, but lost all his money. This made a man of him. With the loss of the money, his senses returned, and he now does his day's work as of old, with a cheerful and contented mind.

I knew another young man, who was a hard drinker, but otherwise a good sort of a fellow.

BANEFUL EFFECTS OF INTEMPERANCE

He came from Pennsylvania at the time of the excitement to which I have referred, spent all his money, and then came to me and took the pledge for a year. "Well, Father," said he, "if I ever make a strike, I'll settle down." He staked a claim, worked hard for three months, got the prospect in good shape, and sold out for $4,000, before the boom died out. On the 3d of July he came down to town, and fell into the claws of the tiger, losing his fortune. I have remarked that the spendthrift is generally the type of the prodigal, but, using the term prodigal in a higher, though rarely accepted, sense of the word, I would apply it, on the doctrine that extremes touch, to that class of men who prefer money to God Almighty. Among the miners this sort of a being is rare, and obtains access to their company by effrontery alone. He is held in contempt by them, for he would rob Lazarus of the few crumbs that fall to his hard lot. His love of the mammon of iniquity shuts the door of his heart to all the sunshine of this life. With enough money, he is always poor. Adoring his sordid god, he holds in disgust and abhorrence all the works of mercy. Hugging his plethoric pocketbook, he ignores all appeals of charity, which is a strange, empty term in his ear. Such a creature I once met in the San Juan. A strong, healthy fellow, and of a parsimonious habit, he seldom came down from the mines, but remained there year after year, until he had eight or ten thousand dollars to his credit in one of the banks. And when he did come to town he showed no signs of sociability. So completely was he wrapped up in himself, that he shunned his fellow-miners. When he had deposited his money, he returned without delay to the mountains, walking the whole distance, while others hired horses to make the difficult journey. To urgent requests from his old parents for help, he lent a deaf ear. Letters came to me, containing inquiries about his health and circumstances, and when I spoke to him of the duty he owed the authors of his being, it was like pulling a tooth out of his head to extract a dollar from him. For awhile, he grudgingly sent them a paltry sum, and at length abandoned his indigent relatives to the cold charity of a British workhouse. But the wrath of the Almighty overtook him suddenly; for one day he was killed in an accident without warning, and forced to leave the dollars which he had so faithfully hoarded. They fell to the lot of a near relative, who, consecrating them to gross vice, never stopped until he had squandered the last cent of the miser's treasure. Such was the fate of one who may have thought to himself that he had a balance at the banker's enough to insure him against Providence itself. "Accursed hunger for gold! to what dost thou not force poor mortals!"

The saloons did a rushing business and the faro-dealers worked two shifts of eight hours a day. John, like all the old soldiers, had a knack of making friends and acquaintances and was not behind the others in spending his money. He made his debut in town by actually taking the large roll of bills, which he carried with him, and passing it over to the proprietor of the saloon. He then waded into the sea of dissipation, careless of the depths before him. The free lunch, of course, was in the bill of attractions, and kept him from sensible employment. Going at a killing pace in vanity fair, he let but little time pass without its peculiar variety of distraction, and was busily engaged in the downward road to ruin, whenever he was capable of standing up at the bar, and shaking the dice. It was only when, stupefied by the draughts of poison he fell on the sawdust floor, that he paused in his mad career. So dead to shame was the poor fellow that he often lay in a heap on the ground.

At the further end of the saloon was a vacant room, in which odds and ends were jumbled together. To this retiring-room the degraded creatures, who had a dollar in their pockets, or were otherwise good for a drink, were removed for future investments. Here stood in the centre of the room, a ragged billiard table, upon which John was tossed to sleep off his drunkenness. During a spree, which might last ten days, the poor fellow kept moving from the billiard table to the bar, constantly under the influence of the deadly drug.

One morning he failed to put in an appearance. Late in the day the owner of the saloon went into the room and found the unfortunate man in a semi-conscious state, breathing stertorously and apparently dying. A physician was summoned. Upon seeing the man, the doctor ordered him to the hospital, where, after some restoratives and much hard work, he was brought to his senses. When he realized his sad condition, his money lost, and his constitution wrecked, the coming prey of death, his soul was so overwhelmed with terror and despair that pen can hardly depict his agony. He drew from his bosom the pictures of his little grandchildren, and kissing the faces of the absent ones, wept as if his heart would break. It was all he had left, and the bitterness of that hour seemed to be intensified rather than assuaged, by the sight of the sweet, innocent faces. The physician said he could not live; his system was poisoned, and his flesh discolored. He had a gigantic frame and must have been a man of prodigious strength. It was not easy to convince him that he was about to die; but when he realized the truth, and with the deepest contrition had received the last sacraments, he became resigned and faced death as in many a hard-fought battle he had faced it in the sixties. The saloon keeper was kind enough to bear all expenses.

A similar deplorable case which came under my notice illustrates the ruin which the habit of drink produces in men of the best natural parts. The man of whom I speak was past middle life, but still strong and healthy. He was born in Ireland, of wealthy parents, who gave him a first-class education. A trained scholar, he could dash off a Fourth of July oration with as many dazzling tropes and figures as a master of rhetoric. Extensive book knowledge was ripened by long intercourse with the world of business. A brother of his adopted for a career the legal profession, and is now a prominent lawyer in his own state. The subject of my remarks literally drank the share of the inheritance that came to him. When all was gone, and with his loss came the remorse which outlives the worst form of dissipation, he moved west and after some years found himself in the great carbonate camp of Leadville. He was not long there, until he formed a syndicate for the purpose of working a mining property, and upon the sale of the mine, his share netted him $12,000. He resolved to go back to Ireland and lead a reputable life among his friends, but while preparing to put his resolution into practice, his passion for drink got the better of him, and he never got farther than Salida, Colorado, where, for nine months, he drank steadily, and when he sobered up, his money was gone. Disgusted with himself, he fled from the town, went over into Gunnison County and tried to begin life anew. He located some claims, and with a companion, commenced sinking a shaft. For six months they worked hard and during this time, true to his spirit of enterprise, tried to organize another company. He was on the point of accomplishing this purpose, when one day an unexpected explosion occurred in the shaft; his legs were both broken, one eye was blown out, and the other was left with little sight. His face was horribly disfigured and filled with burned powder. With a broken nose added to other disfigurements, he was one of the homeliest looking men at the mines. He was obliged to spend nine months in the hospital under the care of the sisters. During this involuntary retirement he assumed the show of the human form; as a result of much meditation on the four last things, some pious reading and the enforced avoidance of the proximate occasion of his besetting sin, he determined to shun drink.

Leaving the hospital, he repaired to Pueblo, where he secured a position as foreman on a Rio Grande construction train. For a year and a-half, he did not touch intoxicating liquors. One day he had some words with the superintendent, quit work and began to drink once more. Before

IN THE SAN JUAN

he ended this spree in the gutter, the savings of a year and a-half were squandered, and the weak creature fleeing from his friends, was forced to beat his way to the San Juan country. Broken in spirit and body, he came to me and begged something to eat. I gradually drew him out and learned his history. I procured him some light work in Ouray and when he regained his strength sufficiently, a position in a mine, where, for nine months, without losing a day, he worked faithfully. But, as the absence of the vice does not prove the presence of the virtue, he was not reformed, the demon of drink held him in his strong, fast hold, and the first day he came down from the mine he inaugurated a new spree, which closed with the delirium tremens. He was, indeed, a sad and pitiable sight. We all encouraged him to cheer up and try again. He did so, and worked about four months, when, on the 17th of March, he came to town and this time fell lower than ever. I was not aware that he was in Ouray, for when drinking he never came near me. About the middle of May I went to Denver on business. During my absence, the ambulance one morning drove up to the sisters' hospital, a man was carried in on a stretcher, and the sister in charge recognized a former patient. He had been on a prolonged debauch and finally lay down by the river to die alone, not wishing after his scandalous behavior to approach priest or sisters. He was tenderly placed on a bed, which was a rare delicacy for him. The heavy breathing and flushed countenance told the experienced sister that he was about to die, so she informed him that he must have a priest at once. The nearest priest was at Montrose and, accord-

BANEFUL EFFECTS OF INTEMPERANCE

ingly, he was wired to come up on the evening train. The poor man prayed all day for forgiveness of his sins, deplored sincerely his unhappy life and strove to make amends for the past in the few hours still left him. As the shades of evening and death drew on, he sank rapidly. He called for the priest again and again. His gentle nurse soothed him and calmed his fears, telling him that the train would soon arrive with the priest. At last, the long, loud whistle of the locomotive, steaming into the depot, reached his ear, and raising his faint voice, he cried out, "Thank God, thank God the priest has now come," and with a cry for mercy on his lips he died, manifesting every sign of true repentance. Next day I came home and we buried the victim of the accursed drink habit at the foot of those rock-ribbed mountains, from whose side trickles down the undiluted waters, which are the beverage of the wise. What a mockery of the end of the drunkard is the musical chant of the gurgling stream as it keeps its way from the mountain passes to the ocean, and what a commentary upon the evils of intemperance is such a wasted career! Man was created with noble faculties, an intellect to pursue truth and a will to love good. But what does the intemperate man care for truth? See him, leaning against a lamp post, swaying to and fro or wallowing in the mire! Ask him what he is doing, or who he is. The answer is a stammering demand for a drink. If he meets a refusal, he does his best to mumble a curse or an oath. Loving his shameful appetites, the time he spares from the bottle he devotes to the neglect of the duties of his state of life. Instead of providing a home for his family, he gives his earnings to the grog shop, and suffers his children to run wild. Disorder prevails at his pretense of a home, where squabbles and blows sometimes end in murder. How does the intemperate man fulfil his obligations to society? He owes the grocer, butcher, milkman, in a word every one he deals with, and when he dies, he leaves the state an impoverished, vicious offspring. The children of the drunkard's home swell the ranks of vice, crowd the reformatories and fill the lunatic asylums. Ah, "what a piece of work a man is! How noble in reason, how infinite in faculty, in form and moving, how express and admirable; in apprehension how like a god, the beauty of the world, the paragon of animals!" This is the temperate man who, with his intelligence developing in the right line, marches swiftly to his end and glorifies his Maker. Alas, what a contrast is the intemperate man, who staggers through life to an inglorious end. Possessed by the demon of drink, "he will not serve;" he scorns advice and resents well-meant friendship; he ridicules the simple lives of his fathers, who in simplicity, became saints. How to satisfy his animal nature, is the absorbing aim of his besotted existence. If only the world were an open bottle, his happiness would be complete. It is by faith, hope and charity that we apprehend God, as it is by the senses we are put into relations with the material world. But the intemperate man believes in whiskey, puts his trust in whiskey, loves whiskey and everything that ministers to a sensual life. The cardinal virtues are the hinges upon which life revolves. Suppose the life of the drunkard is tested by this standard, the conclusion must be

BANEFUL EFFECTS OF INTEMPERANCE

that it were better for him never to have been born. He goes to destruction with his eyes open, his motto is: "Let the last man pay the last man." For the virtues, which should adorn man, he possesses all the vices enumerated by the apostle as the works of the flesh; he is proud, and has nothing but his shame of which to be proud; thirsting for the most brutalizing pleasures, he envies his fallen brother, with whom he regrets he cannot change places. The drunkard is outside the pale of redemption, "Drunkards shall not inherit the kingdom of God." Statistics throw a lurid light upon the appalling evils of intemperance. An analysis of the causes that led in 1890, to the arrest of 7,386 persons, discloses the fact that in 5,096 cases, or three-fourths of the whole number, drink was the responsible cause. The total output of 44,031 breweries in 1894 was 5,475,000 gallons, a number which imagination cannot realize. In that year the consumption of liquor in the United States alone was 1,150,000 gallons. Truly it is a dismal picture, and the reader may ask if there is any hope for the drunkard. I answer yes, but the way to temperance for the habitual drunkard is steep and rocky. Thank God there is a sufficient number of recoveries from the serfdom of drink to prove that a good will with the proper physical and moral remedies will effect a permanent cure. I am not an advocate of total abstinence, and I believe that there are cases in which it may not be necessary to recommend this practice; but some persons are in conscience bound neither to take, touch, or taste the forbidden cup.

I met on my missions another man who had been a heavy and constant drinker for thirty years. He was an old soldier and possessed a fair degree of intelligence. From a large experience, acquired in a military career of five years, he understood men and things pretty well. Before enlisting, he married, like many who are now going to fight the Spaniards. While awaiting the summons to active service, he fell into the habit of drinking to the point of intoxication. When discharged from the service, instead of forsaking his evil way, he went from bad to worse. Of course, when a man drinks to excess, he neglects his business, and as he does not mind his shop, his shop does not mind him. When poverty comes in at the door, love flies out at the window. So this young man, spurned by his relations, and threatened by his wife, left the latter and two children, and fled to the west. His intentions were good, he meant to reform, and then send for them. Perhaps he thought it was a change of climate and not a change of mind he needed. "But a man's mind to him a kingdom is," and no man is at home unless he is at home with himself. His resolutions were weak, and in a strange country he sank lower and lower. After a night's debauch, he swore that that was his last, but before night he would find himself again in the mire. Thirty years of such an existence, away from home and children, is an awful account in the history of a husband and father. This was the man, gray from age and dissipation, that I encountered. It was my special blessing to have been the means under heaven of reforming him and restoring him to his family, to a struggling wife and children, and even grandchildren, who had learned to lisp the name of the unfortunate grandpa, who was going

BANEFUL EFFECTS OF INTEMPERANCE

to ruin in the west. It was on one of my sick calls that I found him like a maniac laid on a bed, strong straps binding his wrists and his ankles pinioned to the posts. He was foaming at the mouth like a vicious dog. One moment horrid despair sat upon him, the next, his eyes set in his head from hideous fright, he filled the watchers with dread. Often calling up all his remaining strength, he vainly endeavored to break the cords which bound him and destroy his enemies. The furies blocked his vision and he shivered with delirious terrors. Cold sweat flowed down his pallid temple, and he caught his breath, as if a mountain's weight lay upon him. The flesh on his face became livid, changing from purple to black, and his cries, moans and howls were unearthly. It was a dreadful presence to witness and the doctor said that there was no hope for him, for he was rapidly passing into a stage of alcoholism out of which few ever come alive. We all prayed that he might reach a lucid interval during which he would be capable of receiving the sacraments. He was a man, however, of great strength and in the mortal combat, the alcoholic poison slowly wore out, and reason once more appeared in a being, who we all believed, was beyond the pale of human or divine salvation. He received the sacraments after due preparation with devout dispositions, and promised God never again to touch liquor. We made up some money for him and sent him to Denver. I am satisfied that his repentance was sincere, and I believe that from that day to this, a period of eight years, he has not tasted a drop of intoxicating liquor. Wonderful action of the Holy Spirit!

IN THE SAN JUAN

> When once Thou visitest the soul,
> Truth begins to shine,
> Then earthly vanities depart,
> Then kindles love divine.

About three years after that awful sick-bed scene, the old man came to me and said: "Father, I want to go home. Will you write to my wife and try to reconcile her to me? Tell her that I am reformed and that I have made a considerable sum of money which will keep us the rest of our lives." In accordance with his request, I wrote in substance: "*Dear madam:*—You will no doubt be surprised to learn that your husband is still alive. For three years he has led the life of a good Christian. He has a competence sufficient to keep you both in your old age. He impresses me favorably, and is a bright, intelligent man, having none of the hardness or cynicism, which dissipation usually produces. I hope you will forgive and forget the past, and only remember the young loving couple, whose hands and hearts were united at the altar in 1861, when he was about to go to the front with the boys in blue. Drink was the cause of all his trouble, but his affection for you is undiminished. Think of the pledges that you mutually made on your happy wedding day, and receive him with open arms. You will be all the happier if you must do a little violence to yourself to fulfil what I believe is under the circumstance a duty." I am happy to to say that the old lady, who hesitated a little through fear of a relapse on the part of her husband, finally achieved a victory over her natural distrust and by the grace of God welcomed to her home the wanderer. I am also pleased to have the assurance that the old man, home again with wife, children and grandchildren, has kept his solemn pledge and leads a useful life, witnessing to the patience of God with sinners. May this example of a remarkable conversion help every unfortunate victim of drink to seek peace where only peace can be found, in a life of temperance.

TENTH SKETCH

IN the winter of 1890 the whole mountain region lay under a blanket of snow, and the narrow trails beaten out by the patient burro, were the only highways a great part of the season. Mother Cline, a celebrated snowslide on the Ouray road, had come down and filled the canon to a depth of fifty or sixty feet with great pines and enormous boulders. Travel was dangerous from Ouray to Red Mountain, and for fourteen miles on the opposite side of the range to Silverton. In the spring, which at this altitude begins about the 1st of May, only the mail carrier will ride a horse over the trails. Snowslides creep silently at first down the mighty slopes and suddenly, with an awful roar, overwhelm the unsuspecting victim. When the snow begins to thaw, the crust becomes rotten, and horses and burros break through it.

On the 27th of April I received a summons to a sick bed from Rico, a mining camp far out in the Dolores country, and over 100 miles from Ouray. The man who bore the despatch had ridden forty-five miles across two ranges of mountains, and over roads where five to six feet of snow, ice, slush and high drifts obstructed his passage. The wires were down and the message did not reach me until Tuesday evening at five o'clock. I lost no time in setting out for Dallas, which is fourteen miles north of Ouray, believing that I might proceed by stage from Dallas to Telluride, and by Trout Lake to Rico. What was my surprise when I found that no stage ran from Telluride to Rico. I returned from Dallas to Ouray, arriving at eleven p. m. and perplexed as to the

TEN DAYS ON A SICK CALL

course to pursue. Saturday, Sunday, Monday and Tuesday—the man must be dead; he was dangerously sick of pneumonia—I could not be home by Sunday. Could I get to Rico at all? These were the thoughts that occupied my mind, as midnight approached. Duty, I exclaimed, and hurrying to the livery I ordered my horse and saddle for half past five in the morning. The Sisters of Mercy packed my vestments for holy mass on the coming Sunday. The holy oils, the chalice, the wine and bread were put away in my grip, and all the necessary preparations were made for the journey. At five o'clock I said mass in the little stone chapel, and a quarter to six found me seated on a good snow horse, which means one that will take it easy when he sticks in the snow and wait patiently until you dig him out. Old Gray, who had lost one ear in a snowslide, and always played lame when tired, humped his back as he began to climb the mountain, the crest of which marked thirteen miles from home. Here, where the little city of Red Mountain nestles among the pines, I was to turn my faithful friend loose and head him for Ouray, which he rarely failed to find. We got along very well until we came to the little park near Ironton. It was still quite dark, and the morning was crisp and cold. The snow was hard and the only danger was in the deep holes in the road. Old Gray managed to escape for a long time, but at last, despite his cautious movements, slipped and fell into a hole, out of which he could not rise, and as he lay on my leg I could not dismount and help him. He made two or three gentle efforts to get up, and as a trained horse will do, not succeeding, remained quiet. My position was embarrassing and painful; much of the horse's weight was on my leg, grinding me into the frozen ice and snow. I believe it was my long ulster alone that saved the bone from breaking. I kept tugging and twisting the old horse's nose and ear, but he lay stiff as a log in the snow. What was I to do? I was growing faint from pain, and running my hand into my overcoat pocket I discovered my hunting knife, which I had recently cleaned. I cut the crust around my hip, and after nearly an hour's scraping and punching, I was enabled to get from under old Gray, who, during all my labors, never stirred. Once free myself, I soon had him up. By this time it was daylight, and I was on the alert for the rest of the journey.

On my arrival at Red Mountain I sent my gray friend home, and strapping my pack on my shoulders, set out for Silverton, thirteen miles down grade. The sun was hot and reflected its burning rays from the seething masses of snow on the mountain sides. When I reached the depot the bell was ringing for the outgoing train to Durango. Boarding the train I rode to Rockwood, which is forty-five miles from Rico. The stage left there every morning at nine, and when the roads were good, generally made connections with the train going to Durango. Fancy my chagrin when I learned that it took the stage two days to reach Rico! At that season of the year, the roads being bad, sometimes you traveled in a wagon, at other times in a sleigh, and sometimes you were forced to walk. You had to push the wagon or the sleigh to help the fagged horses up the slippery hills, and by way of change you spent hours digging the almost smothered horses out of the soft snow or mending broken harness with rope, twine, or wire. It was the last straw on the camel's back to have to pay seven dollars for the privilege of riding on the stage. With two days more on the road I began to think that the sick man was not only dead, but buried. To render the situation more exasperating I had to remain over night in Rockwood in a hotel made of slabs and logs through which the bitter cold winds came at will. The only attraction of the chamber in which I slept in my leggings, overshoes and great coat, was a square of gaudy carpet on the floor, which seemed to mock rather than give any comfort. In the morning about eight I met the manager of the stage line and begged for a horse. He had no horse to spare, but he had a good strong mule; on its right knee, however, there was a bunch about as large as a man's head, and if I had no objections, I might have the mule to ride to Rico. The price would be the same as on the stage, and he would wager ten dollars that the mule would carry me surely, if slowly, to my journey's end before nine that night. And he did carry me slowly, and as will be seen, very slowly.

I took the obliging manager at his word and was soon seated in my McClellan saddle with my vestments strapped on in regular marching order. The day was beautiful. The sun was already warm and little streams trickled down the cliffs and hills. I knew the road and the short cuts so well that I thought I could not make a mistake, but experience taught me that pride goes before a fall. I saw a short cut which I believed led to the main road a mile from Rockwood. Why not take it? I was in a hurry; time was precious. Upon taking this road I found instead of turning to the left, as I had supposed it would, it veered to the right more and more, and presently I discovered that I was going back to Silverton. Coming to what is called in the west a hogback, I had a view of the surrounding country, and saw the road a mile off. I would not turn back and go over the same road again, but cross the country through the soft snow and fallen timber. I followed the hogback for half a mile, and the traveling was fair, but at the bottom of a little valley into which I descended, I found the snow deep and much water. With a determination born of courage and a strong mule, I pushed ahead, when all of a sudden one of my sources of security failed and the mule disappeared, leaving visible only his head, shoulders and embossed knee. I had broken through the ice; I was in a lagoon. In a moment I was out of my saddle and standing up to my hips in water and mud. The mule, with all his shortcomings, was a good one, and with a powerful lunge came forth from his watery grave. I was in a predicament and rather excited, and the mule was trembling. I looked around for some way out. I saw a house in the distance and a man gesticulating. I waved my hand to him and he approached. He proved to be a Mr. Nary, who assisted me in getting out of the swamp and brought me to his house. To say that the priest and mule were well attended would be putting it mildly. Hay and oats were given to the mule, and of course the priest received a royal welcome. My clothes dried, and a good dinner enjoyed, I was in the saddle again at one in the afternoon with three or four miles to my credit, but still

TEN DAYS ON A SICK CALL

forty miles from my destination. The afternoon was uneventful, the mule putting in some solid work on the bad roads. At dusk I was within fifteen miles of Rico and forging my way along as fast as I could.

The awful darkness, which fell like a pall over the canon and on the misty waters of the Dolores, I shall not forget. The silence was broken at times by the hoarse roar of the snowslide, the short bark of the coyote, and the dismal wail of the mountain lion from some neighboring cliff. But the only fear I had was that the mule might fall. I was riding over ground consecrated by the hardships of the first Franciscans, who hundreds of years before followed the star of empire westward and named the sparkling stream Dolores, sorrowful. Was it for the sense of loneliness which came to the missionaries as they passed the silent ruins on the Mancos, the empty dwellings on the cliff, and the desolate country which once fed happy thousands, they named the stream, Dolores? At last, worn out by my long ride, my limbs cramped and my muscles rigid from constant tension, I beheld lights here and there far up the Dolores, and my heart was filled with joy. The mule seemed to quicken his pace and we were soon at the hotel. It took but a few minutes to locate the sick man, whom I found recovering, at the turning point of a bad case of pneumonia. I met the doctor and Nick Hunt, who had carried the despatch over that fearful road, and was nursing the sick man and keeping up the courage of his friend until the priest should arrive. I heard the sick man's confession and then inquired about the welfare of the community. The doctor told me he had a patient who would not live till morning. I asked: "What is his name?" He replied: "Donovan." I said: "He must be a Catholic from the name." The doctor did not know, but it was useless to see the man as he was asleep, and his life depended on this sleep. "Very well, then," I said, "I must see the man for the very reason that he is so low. I must prepare him for death." I cut the conversation short by calling Nick, who had a pair of shoulders that would fill a door, and a fist like John L. Sullivan's, to accompany me to the doctor's office. The doctor had given the patient a room and a colored man, who weighed not less than 200 pounds, as a guard and attendant. I was not very small myself and we sallied forth into the midnight and were soon tapping at the doctor's office door. The darky peeped out and cried: "Who's thar?" "The Rev. J. J. Gibbons, of Ouray, to see Mr. Donovan, who is dangerously ill," I replied, and pushing the darky aside we walked in. The darky remarked as I passed him: "I think he's a Prosbetyrian, I does," but I declined any further parley with him. Donovan was awake in the other room and burning up with fever. He looked at me wildly, while I drew a stole from my pocket. I held up the crucifix to his gaze; it was enough. He said: "Father, I wish to go to confession. I am so glad you came, I have been longing for a priest." Nick took care of the darky while I was hearing Donovan's confession and preparing him for death. Then we left the office, and soon in the cold room and hard bed at the hotel I was asleep, with no mules or bad roads to trouble me.

In the morning I met my old friend McCormick, a bachelor, who came to Rico in 1881, when the boom was on, built a cabin and located several claims. McCormick's cabin was the warmest and snuggest house in town; everything was as neat as wax, indicating what a comfortable place a willing bachelor may have. Mc had one of those famous chests modeled after the traditional Irish chest, with the exception, however, that the chest in question was his sleeping quarters. In the daytime it served for a lounge, the blankets being stowed within it. At night it was unfolded. The lid with legs suitably fitted to it, answered for one bed, on which I slept when I was in Rico, while the owner slept in the chest proper.

"A chest contrived a double debt to pay,
A bed by night, a chest of drawers by day."

With thick blankets and a blazing fire of pine wood, the cabin was warm the coldest nights. McCormick had been running a tunnel into the mountain for years. Alone he had driven it many hundred feet. Fickle fortune, however, did not smile upon him, and the strike which he hoped to make, remained in a state of possibility. His hopes brightened when the great strike was made on the Enterprise mine, and twelve hours a day were put in forcing his way into the solid granite. During all these years of suspense the grub sack was in a low state, bacon, flap-jacks and a dozen of Kansas eggs for Lenten fare, with a surplus of Colorado potatoes, formed the solids for the ambitious driller in the mine. Now and then, when the larder grew empty, Mc was compelled to work at other mines in order to replenish his vanishing commons and acquire a little capital to buy powder. Whenever I came to

IN THE SAN JUAN

town McCormick enjoyed a few days of feasting on porterhouse steak, ranch eggs, bakers' bread, the best coffee and other things that are reputed delicacies in mountain camps. He was a fair cook and so was I, and the meals we dished up were superior, if not in quality, at least in quantity, to such as are furnished in many a mountain hotel. After supper my genial host lit his pipe, took an old violin from over the door and sat down to discourse sweet music. While not an artist like Paganini, he possessed more than ordinary musical talent and played many difficult pieces at sight, which is a rare thing for a workman. He loved to play the old Irish reels and jigs, and like most Irish fiddlers, kept his feet on the move, beating time. When tired of the fiddle he closed the concert for the evening with some well-sung Irish ballad. When the boys heard I was at Mc's they would call at night to tender their greetings and hear the news from the camps around. I generally ended the entertainment with some devotional practice. Mc was a devout Christian. For twelve years in the mountains around Rico, he had worked hard and tried to make a sale of his property, but failed. He was growing old and suffering from an injury received when a boy, and his sufferings were aggravated by the great altitude at which he lived for so long a time. Scarcity of money, however, prevented him from seeking change of climate. At last, broken down in health, he saddled his little burro, and, packing the necessary furniture, sought an inferior altitude and milder climate near Grand Junction. Years of toil had undermined the splendid constitution of McCormick and he could stand no more; so, like Wolsey on his way to meet the king, Mc rested at a cabin by the wayside, and asked the hospitality of the owner. But after a few days' illness he died, the burro, the violin, the gun and the dog defraying the funeral expenses of one of the noblest men I have met in the far west. May he rest in peace.

The Sunday morning following, a large number of Catholics and Protestants attended religious services which I held at the Grand Army Hall. I announced services for the evening again, and requested the prayers of the congregation for the speedy recovery or happy death of Paul Breffort, a young man who was one of the pioneers of Rico. After many years of prospecting, Paul had struck it, and his young wife and two children were then on the Atlantic on a trip to the old folks at home. Paul had weak lungs and always feared pneumonia, which is so fatal in the mountains. The moment I stood beside his bed I saw death written on his face. With his nerve lost and a look of despair in his glazed eye, I could see there was no hope of his recovery. The poor fellow threw his arms around my neck and wept as he thought of his absent wife and children. I succeeded at length in pacifying him, and bade him employ the time as became a brave Christian. He grew calm and resigned, receiving all the rites of the church with great devotion. Sunday night he died, mourned by every man, woman and child in Rico. I remained over until Tuesday to attend the funeral, at which the ceremonies of the church were carried out with as much pomp as a western mining camp allowed, and grief-stricken Protestants and Catholics accompanied the remains of a good man to the little churchyard.

IN THE SAN JUAN

On the morning of the next day I set out on horseback for Telluride in the company of a Denver attorney. The day, as well as I can remember, was May 3, and the snow, although thawing rapidly, was still very deep on the Meadows. We left Rico at seven in the morning on two stout bronchos, which we were to ride as far as the roads would permit, and then dismiss, to town. My legal friend permitted his horse to return before the roads became very bad, while I kept in the saddle, riding between banks of snow from six to eight feet high in some places. It was hard to move with soft snow, cakes of ice, slushy puddles and big holes, which gave the way the appearance of a honeycomb. Struggling and panting with the effort to hold his feet, at length my horse fell and was unable to rise. At that moment, opportunely enough, a son of the green isle, with a big roll of blankets on his back, came along. I seized the broncho by the head and my hardy son of toil having released himself from the encumbrance of his baggage, took him by the tail, and after considerable effort, turned him straight into the road. As a recompense for the kindly help he lent me, I entrusted the horse to him, requesting him to take the animal back to Rico. Having arranged my pack on my shoulder I moved on and soon overtook "the man of law," who generously shared the burden with me. We tramped over the rough road to Trout Lake, where we arrived in the afternoon. There we met the stage from Telluride, and having dried our clothes and enjoyed a good dinner, we set out for Telluride, which we reached about seven in the evening. I said mass the following morning and gave the Catholics of that little town an op-

TEN DAYS ON A SICK CALL

portunity to make their Easter duty. When at Telluride I used to say mass at Mrs. Margowski's. Ten thirty of that morning found me again in the saddle, pushing on to Marshall Basin, one of the richest silver and gold camps in the world. After riding three or four miles I intended, as usual, to turn back the horse, but a mile and a-half from town, I met a burro train in the snow. It was like the Merrimac corking the bottle of Santiago de Cuba, it effectually stopped me, so I was compelled to back my horse and turn him around towards Telluride and let him go back. Afoot and alone I went up to the summit of the mountain near, the Virginius. On the sunny side of the mountain, miniature snowslides were slipping down at every turn, and in many places on the trail I walked over sixty to seventy feet of snow, with a probability of that mighty mass breaking loose, carrying me for miles to the gulch below, and burying me in a snow tomb, which it might take several years to thaw out. I watched my every movement carefully, for I remembered the incident of the mail carrier who was carried away by an avalanche one Christmas eve at a point near the Ophir range. It was hinted that he had left the country with the Christmas presents that came from home to friends in the mountains. Money is a prolific source of evil in thought as well as deed. But the mail carrier's friends were mistaken in their suspicions, for three years later their theory of his sudden departure was exploded, when they found the honest fellow on the farther side of a lake in the shade of a hill frozen in snow and ice, and faithful to his trust, with the mail bag still strapped to his back. As I struggled along with my ulster and grip, for I had

IN THE SAN JUAN

sent my vestments ahead on the stage, I was nearly prostrated by the terrible heat. At two in the afternoon I attained the topmost point of the pass. It would shake the nerve of the strongest to pass through a country of gulches in which a mountain of snow suddenly came crashing along, snapping trees in twain and carrying immense boulders in its course. The ear constantly caught the reverberating tones of distant snowslides, and far up the giddy heights desolation and solitude reign supreme.

In this gateway of the Rockies I knelt down in the snow and returned thanks to God for his protection in taking me over a passage full of dangers and alarms. I felt hungry enough to take my lunch, and after a while spent in reading the inscriptions that were cut in the rocks, generally proclaiming God's goodness and man's misery, I began the descent to Ouray, thirteen miles down the canon. I moved slowly at first, the frozen snow on the shady side of the mountain being very slippery. Make a misstep and you may be treated to a slide of a mile or two, with a probability of taking fire from friction. As I went down the mountain side the snow gradually became softer. I manœuvred around for short cuts, not following the regular trail, and using the tail of my great ulster for a sled. When going too fast I drew up my feet, employing them as brakes, and before long arrived at Porter's, wet and tired. For the rest of my journey the roads were fairly good, and I reached Ouray early in the evening, having been away ten days on a sick call.

ELEVENTH SKETCH

GREAT dangers are apt to arise on sick calls to the mountain camps, especially in the winter season, which includes a period, extending from the last of September to the first of June. Late in September, the storms of rain and hail, which in the great altitudes are accompanied with thunder and lightning, are hard of realization to a native of the lower country. The rain falls in torrents, the atmosphere is saturated with electricity, and ear-splitting peals of thunder cause the stoutest heart to quail. By the end of spring, it is well nigh impossible to travel over the passes, the road being honeycombed with holes, made by horses, mules, burros and men. When the snow freezes at night, the pass becomes so dangerous, that people venture over it, only in cases of necessity.

It was in such circumstances, that, in early spring, I received a telephone message from the Yankee Girl mine, announcing that C—— had fallen 140 feet down a shaft, and was lying, broken and crushed, at the point of death. The message came shortly before daybreak. Dennis, my trusty Achates, and myself prepared for the journey of nine miles. Owing to the inclemency of the winter, I had not visited Ironton for some time, so I determined to take the vestments, and afford the little household of faith, working at the mines, an opportunity to hear mass, and go to holy communion. I telephoned to Ironton to that effect; and we were soon moving slowly along in the narrow trail on the toll road. The journey was beset with difficulties, as the snow was not hard enough to support us, and the road was perforated with deep cavities, the edges of which were frozen. We slipped into these holes from time to time, and found it troublesome to draw our feet out of them. We had two horses, but were compelled to walk most of the way, and lead the animals. Having arrived after many struggles at Ironton, we left our horses at the livery stable, and proceeded on foot to the Yankee Girl. As we went higher up, the snow became deeper and the road, worse. Many times we fell with the pack of vestments, which Dennis was kind enough to carry most of the way. At last, and, of course, much fatigued, we reached the Yankee Girl and found poor C—— in a sad plight. Most of his bones were broken, and he lay on his bunk, suffering intense agony, but still retaining his senses. It is inspiring to witness the rare patience with which the hardy miner endures pain. The night shift were in bed all around me, and in hearing the confession of the wounded man, I was obliged to make use of special precautions. Seven or eight of the boys, all from Donegal, Ireland, were anxious to go to confession and receive holy communion. There was no convenient place in the house, in which I could hear them. I was to say mass in the long dining room, up and down which the cooks and waiters continually rushed, keeping a deafening clatter of dishes and plates, which made it hard to hear. So I said: "Boys, I will go out to the sunny side of the building, and lean against the wall. You may come out, one at a time, and I will hear your confessions." Standing there, and to the passer-by apparently drinking in the beauty of the mountain scenery,

VIRTUE, THE ONLY NOBILITY

I spent half an hour hearing the young men's confessions. Meanwhile, Dennis was busily engaged, setting up a temporary altar, and making appropriate preparations for the holy sacrifice. After mass, at which the boys all assisted with praiseworthy devotion, I administered the last sacraments of the church to the sick man, who was, presently, taken by a special train to Durango, where the doctors decided that it would be necessary to put him in a plaster of paris cast to keep him together.

Mr. C——, like all his compatriots, was a fine specimen of nature's noblemen. Manly, cheerful and christian, he was intelligent, hardworking and edifying. He was unlike those libels on christianity, who, to be reputed smart, copy the ways of the profane, and vie with scoffers in repeating pert quips and flippant jests about holy things. C—— lived well, and, consequently, died well. I improve this opportunity to say a word in praise of the young men, who came from the Emerald Isle to this country. They are a valuable contribution to our fast-growing population, and, in the best sense, promote the grand destiny of the American people, who, in their cosmopolitan composition, possess little of the boasted Anglo-Saxon, but a great deal of the Anglo-Celtic, element. The future historian will be amused to read the recent nonsense of the daily press, upon the close kinship of Americans and Britons. We are a mighty, independent, inventive people; and do not plume ourselves upon mere matters of descent. The Donegal boys, while industrious and self reliant, never forgot the lessons of the little catechism, which they had learned at home. I pause to remark that no philosopher will ever attain the satisfactory solution of the real problems of life, outside the doctrine condensed in this much-neglected catechism. These boys, knowing that they were created to love and serve God on earth and enjoy Him in heaven, cultivated the theological and cardinal virtues, which constitute the summary of true morality. They were not ashamed of the religion of the greatest heroes of history; and after crossing the ocean, continued to devote themselves to the religious practices of their childhood. When not compelled to work on Sunday, it was their wont to walk down to Ouray, nine or ten miles, and assist at holy mass. They were known for the sobriety of their lives, and the careful observance of the laws of the church. They had in one of the youngest of the boys a model of virtue, and, to some extent, a guardian, who kept a fatherly watch over them, and checked any exhibitions of waywardness among them. How different they were from those young men who frequent barrooms and season their speech with curses and obscenity!

I often asked myself, why these young men were so moral and faithful to their religion. I thought it must be because they came from a country where their fathers had fought and died for the faith, leaving a priceless heritage to their descendants. Living among pseudo-reformers, and listening to the ribald songs and lampoons of Orangemen, they grew strong in the midst of adversity; and their roots, like those of the storm-beaten tree on the mountain, sank deeper and deeper for the opposition they encountered. In an atmosphere of bigotry, and hostility to national freedom, they waxed vigorous and fervent

VIRTUE, THE ONLY NOBILITY

in their love for holy church and her salutary teachings, their mental faculties acquiring a rare acuteness, as they were disciplined in defense of the truth. Great as has been the growth of the church in a land so favorable to it as the United States, it would be much greater if her children lived in strict conformity to her doctrine and admonitions; and the young men, of whom I speak, endeavored to extend the kingdom of God on earth, by the best of all sermons, consistent Christian lives. If they were remarkable for anything in particular besides their religious character, it was for their skill in dialectics and their ready wit. Who has not listened to the glib tongue of the Donegal peddler, and how many have been forced to admit his victory in discussion ! Many a doughty opponent has gone down before his biblical knowledge. Taking his adversary on his own ground, he would rout the latter with his own weapons and on the field of his own choosing. Perhaps, another reason for the solid virtue of these young men, may be sought in the circumstance, that it was in the mountains and glens of the north they had been bred. There was no place in such an environment for luxury and effeminacy. They were inured to toil, content with little, and therefore wise. Few appreciate the truth so beautifully expressed by the poet, that adversity is the befitting cradle of wisdom:

> So, would'st thou 'scape the coming ill,
> Implore the Dread Invisible
>   Thy sweets themselves to sour !
> Well ends his life, believe me, never,
> On whom, with hands thus full forever,
>   The gods their bounty shower.

IN THE SAN JUAN

> And if thy prayer the gods can gain not,
> This counsel of thy friend disdain not—
> Invoke adversity !
> And what of all thy worldly gear,
> Thy deepest heart esteems most dear,
> Cast into yonder sea.

As contrasts serve to enlighten, I will here give an example of the opposite kind of character. That same year, which is the period of my sketch, I think it was during the second week in June, I happened to be at Silverton. After mass, one morning, I received a despatch from Rico, urging me to come on without delay; as a man was dangerously sick there. I took the afternoon train to Durango, where I remained over night, and in the morning, set out to Rico, by way of Rockwood. We had a heavy load of passengers and mail matter.

Rico was then enjoying its second boom. The Enterprise mine, owned by the Schwickheimers, had become one of the great properties of southwestern Colorado. Mr. Schwickheimer had worked for years, sinking a shaft, and many a time to procure the necessary funds, had been obliged to go into the mountains and earn some money, by running a saw mill. His pluck and energy were rewarded, and in my time he had 180 men engaged in the mine, for which he afterwards received $1,000,000 in cash. His success excited others, everyone desired to grow rich fast, and thousands of ambitious miners and speculators were hastening to Rico. Real estate went up 500 per cent., houses and cabins that had been neglected for years were put in repair and everyone had a prospect or two. The rush had begun early in the spring, and merchandise, mining and milling machinery and household effects of every sort lined the way from Rockwood to Rico. Mining experts and commercial travelers were hurrying pell-mell to the scene of new discoveries, the former, to buy and place property, and the latter, to sell their various commodities. Among the notables were big C —— of Denver, and another drummer called "Windy." He was a genial gentleman, whom I had known for some time. Some time before, we had together faced a dreadful storm on the Ouray toll road, when the stage had to be abandoned. We were walking down a very steep place leading to Ouray, on which there was nothing but ice; all of a sudden, the two feet were taken from under my cheerful companion and he fell, with an awful thud, plump on the broad of his back. Desiring to show my sympathy I asked if he were hurt. To my surprise he seemed to be offended by the remark, for he instantly replied, "What do you take me for, do you think that would hurt a *man?*" He was not at all ruffled, but kept the whole crowd in good humor.

At noon, the stage drew up before a partially constructed log house, which had a makeshift of a roof in some thin white canvas. Our stage driver, who hailed from New Jersey, having a keen eye for the main chance and genuine Yankee shrewdness, had taken up a homestead between the two ranges of mountains, put the house partly up, flung in a stove, and was ready to serve meals in any style. Seventy-five cents was deemed reasonable at the wayside in those days, and when a strong, rough meal was dished up hot, no one found fault. The stage driver took the greatest pride in his wife's pumpkin pie, although the pumpkins came in cans from the far east, and pressed them on his guests, commending their rare qualities with an easy flow of wit and humor. He made a typical boniface and did everything to render his hostelry an agreeable place of resort.

Among the passengers on the stage there was a sour-looking character who laughed long and loud at a filthy story, and sneered at everything that related to God or Christian decency. A drink now and then from a long black bottle with a neck as short as the entrance to Santiago de Cuba, increased his hilarity as well as the volubility of his foreign tongue. Like the man on the Appian Way, he felt compelled to reveal himself upon the beloved subject, self—and boastfully proclaimed the infidel's views to the disgust of everyone. No one would suspect that it was only three short years since this blatant specimen of humanity left the cottage of his father and came to this country at the expense of a hard-working brother, whose lamp of life was, at the time, flickering on the upper floor of a rickety boarding house in Rico. He did not let the passengers know that this brother of his was then lying ill, but interlarded his profane speeches with Munchausen accounts of the mining prospects of his worthy relation.

In crossing the Hermosa, the driver, while making the turn at the bridge, swung the leaders out too far. One of the horses, slipping over the bank, in a moment was in the swift current, and being rapidly drawn under the bridge, was pulling his mate with him, when a passenger sprang from the stage, and with his pocket-knife cut the traces and lines. In an instant the animal was swept under the bridge, and drowned in the raging torrent. The rest of the distance was made slowly; most of us got out of the coach and walked up the steep hills to lighten the burden of the horses, whose biggest meal in the day is vulgarly called long oats, to wit: the whip. We arrived at the mining camp, just as the candle began to twinkle in the cabin window. A crowd awaited the arrival of the stage at the postoffice, some looking for friends, others for letters, and still others lingering around to gratify their curiosity. Rico, at the time, counted a resident population of some 1,300, but the floating population raised the figure 1,000 more. Everyone had a little money and the people were rushing around, upon business bent. The streets were thronged with men, who were desperately earnest in pursuit of one pet scheme or other, and there were not a few, who, like Micawber, were waiting for something to turn up. The class of promoters is always well represented in a mining town. They sometimes make a sale, or as it is called, a turn, but generally live from hand to mouth. They seldom succeed, for they have neither the experience, the ability, nor the perseverance, of the man who has a vocation for mining. Here also congregate the confidence men and thieves, who flock to new camps, trying to make something out of nothing, and have an easy time. The hotels were full, and beds were at a premiun. Upon the first rush, an enterprising firm came from the east, and erected a showy hotel, which had very fine appointments for a mountain town. It was three or four stories high, and had winding stairs and some handsome furniture. Waiters in flashy costume stood behind the chairs in the ordinary, and pushed them under you with such a sharp jerk that you felt as if you were about to fall on your back; the napkins were done up in triangular shape and the bill of fare was in the approved fashion. The swell style of the whole concern nearly paralyzed the miners, who are men of simple ways; it was not long until it paralyzed the firm, too, for the tall price and the airy menu soon drove the hotel's patrons to the less aristocratic boarding house and its substantial meals.

Having alighted from the stage, I lost no time in seeking the sick man. He was very ill, but had enough of strength left to make a long fight, and perhaps recover. I heard his confession and promised to bring him the holy communion in the morning. I then betook myself to McCormick's neat cabin, which was always open to the priest. Next morning, I said mass and prepared the sick man for death, as he showed signs of growing weaker. During the day, I was apprised that a mother and her baby were ill at the springs on the West Dolores; I was requested to come to see them. I visited most of the Catholics in the camp, and we considered plans for building a church. Accompanied by a brother of the sick woman, I left Rico the next morning for the West Dolores. The air was fresh and bracing, and the ride of eighteen miles was a mere pastime. On the high plateau, called the Meadows, over which we rode, the grass was stealing up through the cold ground, still soggy from the enormous snowfall of the previous winter. We met a man riding a chestnut horse, which threw out one of its fore feet, and I remember I called the attention of my companion to the beauty and

VIRTUE, THE ONLY NOBILITY

military step of the animal. The horseman wore a Mexican sombrero and seemed to eye us with suspicion, but we passed on without speaking. That same day, and about the same hour, one of the greatest bank robberies in the history of the state occurred at Telluride, about thirty miles from where we then were. The robbery was well planned and executed, and the stranger on the chestnut horse was, perhaps, on his way at that moment to join his companions, who were riding with the booty for dear life. For several weeks before the robbery, three men had been camping on the mesa south of Telluride. They had four horses, one of which was used to pack the camping utensils and cumbersome baggage. The horses were well fed with oats, and blanketed every night, something unusual for ordinary cowboys to do. Every afternoon they rode into town, took a few drinks, smoked good cigars and were social companions for the miners. Upon these visits they learned all that was necessary about the bank, ascertained the pay day of the miners, and resolved to hold up the cashier. At that time there were 400 or 500 men working in Marshall Basin, and on the day when the miners were paid, a general holiday was observed. When the day arrived the three men came to town on horseback, a circumstance which no one would notice, and after reconnoitering for some time, went to a saloon, where they took only a cigar each. The day before $22,000 had been sent to Telluride, and was in the regulation time safe. At twenty minutes to ten, the cowboys again mounted their horses, rode past the bank, and, I presume, saw that the safe was open. Wheeling around in the square, they withdrew to an alley, where they dismounted, tightened their saddle girths, remounted, and rode back to the bank. One remained in the saddle and held the horses of the other two, who strolled leisurely into the bank, as if to draw money, or make a deposit. The bookkeeper was just leaving the bank with a package of letters for the postoffice, so that only the cashier, who was also teller, was in at the time. Not a soul was near, when the tall, dark robber stepped up to the teller, and bade him throw up his hands. That official turned around, looked at him and began to laugh, but before the laugh left his face the man on the outside pushed the long barrel of a revolver almost into his mouth, and with an awful oath threatened to kill him. The cashier's hands went up at once, and the other robber sprang over the railing and quickly emptied into a gunny sack the crisp greenbacks that were stacked on the counter, as well as all the gold that was at hand. From the piles of silver he took only a few dollars. The affrighted cashier was informed by the robber who was guarding him, that he had a mind to kill him, as a coward is not fit to live. They warned him to keep quiet, and give no alarm; and, with this caution, the pair of daylight robbers walked out of the bank. Strange to say, during the whole transaction there was not a man in sight. The coolness of these men may be judged from the remarks of the tall dark one, who said, "Boys, the job is well done, and we have plenty of time, keep cool now and let us be gone." Once in the saddle, they rode up the street, shooting off their guns, as a warning, no doubt, to all who might try to capture them. The sheriff of the county

VIRTUE, THE ONLY NOBILITY

was standing in the courthouse door when they rode by, hooting, yelling and firing off their revolvers. He declared if he had had his horse he would follow and arrest those notorious cowboys. The cashier, growing bold, took a peep out; and finding the coast clear, stepped into the street where he met the bookkeeper, who was returning from the postoffice. The former was as pale as death, trembled from head to foot and with a mighty effort, stammered out: "*I-t-s-a-l-l-g-o-n-e.*" Fifteen minutes after the bank had been looted, twelve men were in the saddle, and away over the hills after the robbers. The pursuit was fast and furious for a few miles, but the grass-fed horses were no match for the grain-fed and well-picked animals of the bank thieves. Arrived at Trout Lake, fifteen miles away, they rested, swallowed big doses of whiskey, and amused themselves by shooting the letters out of the signs. When they beheld the sheriff's posse a short distance away, they mounted again and rode off hastily. The sheriff followed, but some of the horses lay down on the road, and when the Meadows were reached, of the twelve who started, only two or three were able to continue the chase. The others went to Rico to get fresh horses. By this time, the robbers were not far behind us. We met a Swede on the trail about two miles out from the Meadows; he had been looking at his bear traps and was on his way home to prepare his noon-day meal. While thus engaged, the bank robbers came in, and it is said that the Swede cooked the meal for the four in short order style, as one of them, who was under the influence of liquor, followed him around the house with a loaded revolver; however, he gave a twenty-dollar gold piece to the Swede; and, wishing him good day, left in a hurry. In those days, the timber was so thick that one man could defend himself against a dozen. The robbers knew every trail in Colorado and Utah, and a brigade of soldiers would have little chance of arresting them.

We arrived at the West Dolores Springs about noon, and had dinner. I attended the sick call, baptized the child and rendered whatever spiritual aid I could, to the mother, and then we set out on the return trip. There was a light shower at the time, so we made up our minds to shorten the way by crossing the mountains, and make Rico in nine instead of eighteen miles, which was the distance by the road. By doing so, we missed the bank robbers, who about that time were enjoying the enforced hospitality of the Swede.

That afternoon, we passed through some of the finest timber of pine and spruce I had ever seen. Some of the pines were 100 feet high without a limb; indeed, this was one of the primeval forests, where the axe and saw mill had not found an entrance. Going up the shady side of the mountain, we found many feet of snow in the old trail, although it was late in June. Streams were rushing down on all sides, and myriads of beautiful flowers, peering up through the snow, made a pleasing picture. When we reached Rico, all the town was agog over the bank robbery. All the old horses and muskets were brought into requisition, large rewards were offered for the apprehension of the robbers; but not one of them was ever caught. They must have made their way to the Blue Mountains of

VIRTUE, THE ONLY NOBILITY

Utah and may be there yet. The Robbers Roost has long been a thorn in the side of the authorities, and recently, some of these bandits were captured and others killed.

Upon my return to Rico, I went to see my sick patient, who had been neglected in the interval, by his worthless brother, who was a gambler as well as toper. I found the poor fellow weak, but sanguine of recovery. I sat by his bedside, far into the night. During my vigil, the brother, in a state of inebriation, came into the cheerless room, remained only a few moments and departed for his dear haunt, which was a saloon across the way. Before leaving the hopeful man, I informed him that I should be obliged to leave early for home next morning, as it would take two days to get back to Ouray. I encouraged him and promised to call again in the morning, before taking the stage. I bade him good night. Soon I was sound asleep at McCormick's, where the alarm clock startled me at five in the morning. I dressed in a hurry, and, after a while, was on the street to seek the boarding house of the sick man. Up the old decaying stairs, which were built on the outside, I pressed my way. At the second story landing, I found a long dark hall, on the right hand side of which, and near the middle of the building, was the large room in which he lay. I walked in with as little noise as possible. The early dawn was just stealing in through the dusty window, casting a sickening glamor over the pale face and white coverlets, which met my gaze. I approached cautiously and said to myself, "He is sleeping peacefully, and now that the crisis has passed, he will surely recover." I laid my hand on his forehead, and to my horror, found the man was dead. There he was, cold in death, the blanket still drawn around him, but not a soul to close his eyes or stretch out the lifeless form. I went back to McCormick's, procured my ritual and returned to the death-chamber. Lighting the candle, I read the burial service—alone with the dead man, sprinkled the corpse with holy water, and, tearing a leaf from my diary, wrote in substance: "This body has been blessed for the grave," and signed my name. Having pinned the notice on the breast of the deceased I put out the candle, and from the awe-inspiring scene stole quietly away. I was soon on the stage and whirling along the mountain road to Telluride, absorbed in the sober reflections awakened by my latest experience. As I thought of the forsaken brother, dying alone in that dark, cheerless room, I might have well been led to consider that when death comes, a man feels he is alone with God. How true it is that if we desire to have a little of the composure of the higher life in death, we must cultivate much of the loneliness of death in life! It is the part of the wise to live in the face of death.

SILVERTON, COLORADO

TWELFTH SKETCH

IT is said that Colorado will be one of the greatest states in the Union. The unlimited variety of her productions, the salubrity of her climate, and her inexhaustible treasures of gold, silver, coal, iron, marble and stone, insure her future pre-eminence. The resources of other states are few, and many of them have uncongenial climates, but the Centennial state has all the natural advantages of her sisters, and, besides, a population that for enterprise and energy have earned for themselves the significant title of Rust· lers. Some portions of Colorado are barren, yet there is a large part of the state so rich in the precious metals, and having such a high degree of fertility, that she promises to rival the most illustrious nations of the past. What was the city of Denver thirty years ago? A village. Now what is it? A metropolis, and known far and wide as the Queen City of the Plains. The same qualities which have made Denver what it is, have borne similar fruits in other portions of the state; but perhaps nowhere more conspicuously than in the San Juan, where possibilities are revealing themselves, which will place it among the most prosperous sections of the state. Take that tract of land around Durango, Farmington and Fort Lewis. What more fertile soil! What a field of enterprise for the man devoted to agriculture and horticulture! For here will one day be cultivated the vine, which for quality and quantity will vie with the products of the richest vineyards of sunny France. I will reserve, for another part of this sketch, the enumeration of other sources of prosperity, which this region, teeming with plenty, possesses.

Thirty years ago the San Juan was a mere wilderness. With the exception of the hardy trapper and hunter, the white man scarcely ever entered its canons, traveled along its rivers, or over its mountains and dense forests. The tepee of the wild Indian, smoke-colored and tattered, was the only sign of human life, where to-day nature's latent forces are employed in the interests of a progressive nation. Electricity has changed the face of things. By this power the great mining mill has supplanted the old-time water mill. It has taken the place of the coal oil lamp, and, in many cases, the miner's candle. With its brilliancy it has dispelled the faint gloom that formerly hovered over the town and the mine, thus turning night into day. The ground is no longer parched. Swift sparkling springs wind their silvery course through plains, which once were arid. Modern machinery, in skillful hands, has cut channels through which rush the life-giving waters, that convert the desert into a garden. As I gazed upon these first fruits of nature, awakened by science to a new life, there arose before my vision fields of grain rising and falling like waves of molten gold in the setting sun, and a happy population engaged in industrial pursuits and enjoying the fruits of their toil.

"There in full prime the orchard trees grow tall,
  Sweet fig, pomegranate, apple fruited fair,
Pear and the healthful olive. Each and all
  Both summer droughts and chills of winter spare;
All the winter round they flourish. Some the air

Of zephyr warms to life, some doth mature.
Apples grow on apple, pear on pear,
Fig follows fig, vintage doth vintage lure,
Thus the rich revolutions do aye endure."

And as my vision lingered over this scene, Durango, bearing in her hand the horn of plenty, appeared the mistress of the southwest. For location, altitude, climate, mineral and agricultural resources, this city is second to none in southern Colorado, and must eventually become a great center of trade. She has her smelters to treat the train loads of ore that day by day are brought down from Silverton and elsewhere. The waters of the Las Animas River flow through it, furnishing a power that might be conserved for many purposes.

Durango has mild winters. Snowstorms, however, prevail, but the snow melts so rapidly that the tinkle of the sleigh bells is seldom heard in the streets. The atmosphere is not so dry as that of other towns, having an equal elevation. But the climate possesses qualities which build up the broken-down system without weakening the nerves. The valley to the north, on the way to Silverton, is one of the richest and most beautiful in Colorado. It is nine miles in length, and sheltered by red granite walls rising hundreds of feet and shutting out the cold winds of the higher regions. Fruit, vegetables and grain yield large returns, and the opportunities for the ranchman surpass his expectations. Toward the north is one of the most notable watering places in the San Juan. Hither throng year after year multitudes of tourists, the sick, the decrepit and rheumatic, all taking the medicinal waters which boil up from the solid rock. To this fountain of

IN THE SAN JUAN

Perpetual Youth the miner repairs to invigorate his system, impaired by hard work and the nervous tension caused by the high altitude of Silverton and its neighboring mines. Pneumonia is much feared at the mines, and when the first symptoms of the dread disease appear the sick miner at once seeks a low altitude and enters the sisters' hospital at Durango. The miners look upon the hospital as their home in time of illness, and properly, too, because they liberally contributed to its erection, and upon all occasions show their good will toward it.

Some of the mines around Silverton are at an elevation of 12,000 feet far above timber line, and have been worked with profit for several years. Silverton has always been a thrifty mining town. It lies in a beautiful park and is surrounded by very high mountains. It is well laid out and has some large business blocks and many neat cottages, and for those who can bear a dry, cold climate, it is a desirable place to live in. The summer and fall are delightful, and the winters, though cold, are not unpleasant. It has churches and schools, and as I said in a previous sketch, an altar society worthy of great praise for their zeal in the cause of religion. A branch of the Denver & Rio Grande Railroad extends from Silverton to Durango through the Las Animas Canon. As there is a down grade nearly all the way to Rockwood, the brakes are kept well set, and the train is borne along by its own momentum. The scenery is varied, and generally partakes of the sublime. Along the track flows the Las Animas River, the bed of which is strewn with immense boulders, over which the waters dash in their impetuous course. Massive rocks, weighing thousands of tons, overhang the river and the track, and in some places shut out the light of day. In every few miles, tributaries, rushing through the sides of the canon, feed the Las Animas. At intervals along those inaccessible heights, the eye rests upon naked crags and forests of pine, around which are scattered gigantic trees lying prone on the ground. Now the sight of the spectator is refreshed by patches of green sward, and again by mountain flowers, which lend enchantment to the view and clothe the mountain with a varied hue.

What has been said of Silverton may be here repeated about Rico, Ophir and Telluride. Situated in a spacious park, which narrows down into the San Miguel valley, Telluride is a typical mountain town, progressive, and having an enterprising population. Many of the modern improvements are found there, and its pretty residences are set off by the graceful trees which grow along the streets. At some distance may be seen the snow-capped peaks of Marshall Basin, which contain the great mines, which have given Telluride a prosperous community.

Life in the mining regions, especially in the wilds of the San Juan, is little known to eastern people. Indeed, even to most western people it is a land of mystery, for only a few, and these principally miners, go there to seek their fortune. Far away from the Queen City of the Plains, the center of commercial life in Colorado, it attracts only the energetic and the robust, who have the hardihood to endure the severe cold that prevails in those altitudes. Many of her mines discovered and developed within the last fifteen years may be classed among the richest in the world.

IN THE SAN JUAN

The quantity and the quality of the ore extracted from those underground storehouses are such as to surpass even the fabulous wealth of Crœsus. Let me point to the mines of Sneffles Basin, Marshall Basin, the mines of Ophir, the Sunny Side, the North Star and the Yankee Girl of the Red Mountain district. The latter, I was informed, produced $450,000 in the short space of four months. It must not be inferred, however, that nuggets of gold and chunks of silver are picked up by chance on the surface of the mountains. This may be true of some favored locality, but most of San Juan's mines have become rich producers by hard labor, an immense outlay of money, and an endurance of untold hardships. Nevertheless, some of the mines have been discovered at the grass roots, and a few have made fortunes in a very short time. But the locator seldom realizes much from his valuable find, as, generally speaking, hundreds of feet of a shaft must be sunk in the solid rock before a mine pays. To do this, machinery of various kinds must be set up, houses erected, for the construction of which large trees must be cut down, and often hauled up very high mountains, at an enormous expense.

Those who have never seen a mine entertain rather peculiar notions of its workings and general appearance. The mines of the San Juan are what are called fissure veins. Those veins may be traced for a long distance across the country, but ordinarily only in one kind of formation, such as granite, trachyte, quartsite, etc. The vein is found to vary in width, averaging from a few inches to many feet. It is often barren on the surface, or shows a little gold or silver, but may increase in richness, as depth is gained. But it may be a bonanza before even the pick or shovel is used. In deep mines the shafts are neatly timbered, to prevent the accidents that may occur from the falling of loose rocks and caves. Electric light is used in many of the mines, rendering the interior not the gloomy hole which the uninitiated picture to themselves. A cage, resembling the elevator in a hotel, brings you up and down the shaft from one level to another. These levels may be compared to tunnels, and are sometimes illuminated by electric lights. They are excavated on the vein for the purpose of getting out the ore with more facility and bringing it to the main shaft, where it is conveyed to the surface by the cage. Some of the machinery used in these mines costs hundreds of thousands of dollars. In most mines large volumes of water make their way through the rock into the shaft, requiring pumps of the largest capacity to keep out the water and render the mines workable. The number of men employed depends largely on the hardness of the rock, the amount of ore, and the extent of the mine's development. To cut through the solid rock it is necessary to use machine drills, which blacksmiths are constantly engaged in sharpening. To sink a shaft through certain kinds of rock involves a cost as high as twenty dollars a foot, without taking into consideration the expenditure for machinery, hauling and other incidental requirements.

The average wages of miners in the San Juan was three and a-half dollars, until the reduction in the monetary value of silver took place. During the pioneer days the wages paid the miners was much higher. That the miners are a class who are deserving of high wages is evident to any one who reflects upon the many dangers and hardships to which they are subjected. The miner is no time server "amid these mountains old and gray." He is a freeman, and perhaps enjoys a larger measure of independence than most men. By sinking his shaft deeper on his prospect, or lengthening the tunnel, he pays his yearly taxes to Uncle Sam.

In the mining camps cabins are constructed of logs of spruce or pine, hewed smooth by the keen adz to fit closely, then the chinks are filled with mountain mortar, which is a protection against the intense cold of that region. The old fireplaces, similar to those which our forefathers built on the frontiers half a century ago, may still be seen along the streams of the San Juan falling into decay. They are sad reminders of a generation that is passing away. If married, the miner lives with his family in camps, villages and cities like Durango, Silverton or Ouray. Their homes are neat, and in them are found all the comforts of life, comforts sometimes even bordering upon luxury. He is a good liver, there being nothing small or miserly in him. Work and location require that he should eat well. The nervous tension at such an altitude has such an effect upon body and mind that the best food is indispensable to supply the rapid waste that is continually going on. In order to blast the solid rock it is necessary to drill deep holes. This is done by one man striking on the drill while the other is turning it. Such work demands no small amount of muscular force, hence the necessity of good, substantial food. Vegetables, such as radishes, onions, lettuce, beets and carrots, grow at an altitude of 9,000 feet, while potatoes and cabbage are raised at an inferior altitude, or may be bought at reasonable prices from the ranchmen in the valleys.

The miner is nature's student. His special delight is to examine the various rocks and discuss the different formations. The geological knowledge he displays would do credit to some of our noted scientists. He is acquainted with modern theories concerning the origin of the precious metals. And it would seem that the lofty peaks by which he is surrounded make him a man of broad views and noble ideals, and as the nature of his pursuit in life causes him to travel around from one mining country to another, he has a practical knowledge of geography and an experience which make him quite an interesting fellow. He is possessed of a sound judgment and a critical mind which place him above the average man, though he may not understand formal logic; in short, he is the embodiment of good nature and sociability.

The Denver & Rio Grande Southern Railroad has built from Telluride to Vance Junction a branch, which makes connection with the main line on the San Miguel River. *Canon* would be a more appropriate name than *valley*, for this wide chasm in the Rockies, as there is little vegetation, and the ranches are few and small. Gold in fair quantities has been discovered at Saw Pit and close to Placerville. Some eastern syndicates put up large plants of machinery, but receive small returns for the vast sums invested. On either side of the canon the red sandstone walls rise to great heights. On the right as you go down the stream is the San Miguel Plateau, rich in all that makes a great stock country, while on the mesas to the left are Gypsum Valley, Paradox Valley, Basin Plateau and Island Plateau. A finer country could hardly be desired. The land is quite level around Wright's Springs, and is irrigated without difficulty. The San Miguel waters this vast region, which also contains many small streams, not yet named on the maps. Here the deer and the elk winter and bask in the sunshine, while the north wind pierces the traveler on the mountains above. Grand Junction, which is on the border line of this sparsely settled country, is a well-known market of peaches, apples, grapes, and other varieties of fruits. Even people outside the state have heard of Grand Junction Peach Day, which is a yearly celebration of the wonderful productiveness of this section of the San Juan. There is a vast acreage of wheat, corn and other cereals in the Grand Valley, where Grand Junction stands. There is not a sufficient rainfall to insure regular crops, but the system of irrigation, which has been introduced in recent years, is complete and effective. Large farms are now watered at the proper time and in a few hours. The water is supplied from the main ditch, which is built on the highest ground and regulated by headgates, which can be readily opened or shut. A single acre has produced fifty bushels of wheat or eighty bushels of oats. Generally, the returns compare favorably with those of the best tilled lands of the east.

Coming up the Gunnison River from Grand Junction, the first town that greets the traveler is Delta. It breaks on the eye bright and cheery and drives away all the dreary impressions left by the sand hills, jagged rocks and desert land that skirts the river for many miles. At Delta this gloomy canon spreads out like a fan to the foothills. Here the Uncompaghre and the Gunnison form a junction, and the whole valley is well settled. Many of the ranchmen are wealthy, and all have comfortable homes.

In a southeasterly direction, thirty-five miles from Montrose, and in the canon of the Uncompaghre, nestles Ouray, the picturesque. The Uncompaghre is one of the most beautiful and fertile valleys in the San Juan, and so favored by nature that Uncle Sam regarded it as a good site for a fort. Here Ouray, the chief of the Utes, built an adobe house, where he lived in peace with his charming Chipeta. The ruins of this house still exist, and are pointed out to the traveler, a memorial of a vanishing race.

Shall I describe Ouray? No. This task I will leave to a poet priest, a dear friend of mine, who, during a short sojourn there, was so enraptured with the city and its surroundings, that he was moved to sing its praise in these exquisite lines:

> There's a spot among the Rockies,
>   In Colorado's wilds,
> Where the breezes whisper music
>   And the midday sunlight smiles,
> Where the mountains like grim wardens
>   Keep watch both night and day
> Where nature's hand has placed them
>   The guardians of Ouray.
>
> Do you journey thro' the canons,
>   Twixt high and rocky walls,
> And listen to the murmur
>   Of busy waterfalls?
> Are you seeking health or pleasure
>   'Mid the mountains old and gray?
> You'll find the yearned-for treasure
>   In picturesque Ouray.

IN THE SAN JUAN

Do nature's pictures tire
  And the murmuring of the rills,
Do you long for something homelike
  Amid the towering hills?
Seek ye a place to rest in
  Where gentle calm holds sway
To soothe the weary spirit?
  You'll find it in Ouray.

FINIS.

www.ingramcontent.com/pod-product-compliance
Lightning Source LLC
Chambersburg PA
CBHW071703090426
42738CB00009B/1648